HEALING PRAYER

*For the sick, injured,
abused, marginalized, depressed,
sinful or deceived. And anyone else.*

HOW TO DO IT.
WHAT TO AVOID.

GEORGE BYRON KOCH

שְׁמַע יִשְׂרָאֵל ה' לֹאהֵינוּ ה' אֶחָד

SHEMA ISRAEL, ADONAI ELOHEYNU, ADONAI ECHAD
HEAR, O ISRAEL, THE LORD OUR GOD, THE LORD IS ONE.

AND YOU SHALL LOVE THE LORD YOUR GOD
WITH ALL YOUR HEART, SOUL AND STRENGTH.
THIS IS THE FIRST AND GREAT COMMANDMENT.

THE SECOND IS LIKE IT:
YOU SHALL LOVE YOUR NEIGHBOR AS YOURSELF.

ALL THE TORAH AND THE PROPHETS
STAND UNDER THESE TWO COMMANDS.

WITH GRATITUDE FOR THESE COMMANDS, AND OUR CREATION...

Preface

Unless otherwise noted, Scripture is taken from *The Holy Bible*, New King James Version (Nashville: Thomas Nelson, 1982).

Greek & Hebrew definitions and transliterations are from *BibleWorks Software for Biblical Exegesis and Research*, electronic edition of the Bible (Bigfork, MT: Hermeneutica, 2001).

Sourced from "Teaching Healing Prayer for the Victims of Sin," a doctoral project, copyright 2003 by George Byron Koch.

Byron Arts Publishing
www.ByronArts.com
Copyright 2023 by George Byron Koch. All rights reserved.

ISBN 978-0-9777226-9-3

Cover Design by Praloy Saha
Praloy.saha30@gmail.com

Copy Editing and Layout by George August Koch
GeorgeAugustKoch@me.com
CopyEdit.pro

Additional materials and resources available at:
GeorgeKoch.com

Thanks and Acknowledgments

This book began as a doctoral project some two decades ago, then titled "Teaching Healing Prayer for the Victims of Sin." The main theme then was healing and restoration for victims of abuse and oppression, and teaching *how to do this* for congregations and individuals. Much has grown and changed since that time, and the insights gained have proven applicable to all forms of suffering and healing—physical, spiritual and psychological.

The book is dedicated to the faculty of The King's University, especially Jack Hayford, Paul Chapell and Wess Pinkham, for their energy and insight in creating the Doctor of Ministry program two decades ago, and for allowing me the privilege of being in its first cohort.

Thanks to Leah Coulter, my supervisor, for her ministry, her interest in victims of sin, and her help as I plowed through this work; to Jon Huntzinger, for his careful reading and helpful suggestions for improvement; to the members of my cohort, who challenged me and took challenges as they lived with me with authenticity and integrity, particularly Jim Robb, who touched (or thumped) each of us with his passion, but who stepped from this life into the next before he could finish this course of study with us.

Thanks also to "Gracie," a friend, pastor, and mentor in seminary, whose own view of God's character and His willingness to heal were transformed when she willingly subjected herself to my first attempt at healing prayer and was suddenly and profoundly healed of lifelong and severe rheumatoid arthritis. We were both surprised by God and set on a course of learning more of His healing touch and sharing it with others. You'll read more about this as the book begins.

Church of the Resurrection (now renamed New Jerusalem House of Prayer) has been my spiritual home since my ordination, and it is truly a place of the priesthood of all believers. I have learned so much and experienced so much in the presence of so many people so gifted in hearing from the Lord and so willing to be ministers of His healing power. It is an extraordinary honor to serve there.

Of particular note are the early training materials and teaching expertise of Margaret Webb and Randy Fisk, both insightful and caring leaders; the teaching and prayer-team leadership of Linda Eiserloh, Mary Beth Campbell, Lynn Bowman and Cynthia Bauman; Jessica Handy Duisberg, now a leader in Immanuel Prayer of Alive and Well; Rev Dr Sharon Lewis and Amazing Love Healing Ministry, and the many other prayer-team, staff and congregation members who contributed regularly to our training and ministry. The list is long and filled with grace and generosity!

In the challenge of shared ministry, the foundation on which healing is done, thank you to Rev Dolores Wiens, Rev Ben Tumuheirwe, and Rev Ray Waterman, for wisdom and faithfulness in caring for our flock, and Cheryl Waterman and Randy Fisk, for music and worship to inspire our souls.

Pastor John Skarphol of Glad Tidings in Fargo, North Dakota, which hosted our teams during our healing-prayer conference, was proven to be not just a friend, but more like a brother I had worked with all my life. Along with his wife, Nancy, Pastor Karen Nelson, and Lori Neer, John and his team made our stay sweet and Spirit-filled.

Terry Brady helped organize the many books and other resources consulted in preparing this book.

Holly Holmberg created the entries for the index, bibliography and glossary.

Praloy Saha created the cover art, winning a design contest over a dozen other artists. Thank you for its beauty.

My family has done more than put up with me in my pursuit of my doctoral degree and later my work on this book. They love me and encourage me and make me do things I need to do but am too thick-headed to do without their nudges. Thank you to George, Isaiah, and especially my beloved wife, Victoria. I could not be more blessed than I am by your life in mine.

A special additional thanks to son George August Koch, a professional writer and editor of extraordinary talent (he makes words sparkle while retaining the "voice" of his authors), for his work and counsel on this and so many other projects. He is so good at it, it's downright scary.

And to my parents, George and Patricia (now in heaven), thank you for encouraging me and guiding me in life, even when it was really, really hard.

Maggie, our parish administrator, has been faithful over decades. Her calm, thoughtful and thorough work makes our congregational life simpler and more understandable.

Judy Davis has been a deacon at my side for many years. Her confident, constant support and help have been invaluable.

Rebecca Teguns has served as "Associate Pastor" for many years, but the truth is that her insights, energy, prophetic calling and deep friendship have been more than helpful. They have been life-giving.

The truth is that many minds, hands and hearts, over the course of years upon years, have combined to make this book and its content, all of which owe their contribution to the leading of the Holy Spirit.

And finally, happy thanks to Deanna, Shelli and Trish from Stardust Bowl, where I camped out and worked on this book while my son Isaiah bowled. The ladies made Stardust an ideal place to work hard without disruption.

TABLE OF CONTENTS

1.
Real Healing From the Real God

This is a book on healing—how God does it and how you can be a catalyst for it. This may sound silly to some, frightening to others, but it is normal in Scripture, and even the least "worthy" of us can be healed—and also be used by God for the healing of others.

"Healing" here includes physical healing, of course, but it also goes beyond that into healing for emotional wounding and spiritual disease, healing for victims of violence and abuse, healing for damage done by those who should have been trustworthy leaders but instead perpetrated harm. God can bring healing and freedom from the past to each and every one.

Not only will you discover here the rich history of healing, and the testimony of Scripture about it, but you will also hear stories of real people with real diseases and injuries who receive real healing. These stories are told by people who were there and witnessed or received it firsthand. They are not lab experiments or clinical trials, and the stories are not proofs. They are testimonies. Yet each one is real, from a real person, who experienced real and inexplicable healing.

More, they are not randomly gathered from "out there," where stories abound but true witnesses seem to be mere mists. These are either people I know and whose healing I personally witnessed, or people whose healings were witnessed or received by close and trusted friends of mine, who shared the stories with me as accurately as they could.

The first is one I personally witnessed. For the privacy of those involved, I have changed names and locations here and elsewhere, but my telling is as truthful as possible. You can read the other stories in Appendix A, "Stories of Real Healings." Do. They will give you courage. Now, to begin…

It was the first time I ever prayed for healing.

I was a trainee at a pastors' program about visiting hospitalized people. In this program, I was with instructors and other trainees who believed God no longer did miraculous healings like the ones in the Bible. People who believed such things were regarded with condescension and suspicion, or at best casually disregarded. I was one of those people who believed God still healed, and I was viewed with skepticism.

I often argued with both trainers and trainees that I believed God still supernaturally intervened and healed people. But I was new to ministry, inexperienced, and I had the unfortunate disadvantage of never having personally witnessed what I believed to be true. You can imagine some of the debates.

Our training consisted primarily of learning how to talk with people who were hospitalized, depending on their disease, or injury, or whatever. That may sound odd, but the truth is we often don't know what to say to someone who is in the hospital, or even at home and gravely ill. Platitudes are useless, and we might say something dumb or even hurtful ("You still have cancer because you lack faith. Pray harder"). Pastors get called to hospital beds all the time, so it makes sense that they get instruction in what to do and say.

We were told *not* to pray for healing. Ours was to be a "ministry of presence," meaning just to be a chaplain who is present with the person. No more. Prayer for comfort was okay, even prayer for wisdom for the doctors, but *not* for healing. Perhaps it was because the trainers' theology didn't believe such supernatural healing possible; perhaps it was to not set expectations that would be dashed; perhaps it was to avoid liability. I'm not sure.

After we visited patients, we wrote up our encounters in what were called "verbatims," shared them with our supervisors and other trainees in small groups, and got feedback on how well they thought we'd done.

We also did "role-playing" where one trainee would pretend to be a patient, and another would be the pastor/chaplain. The "patient" would be told what disease or injury they had—out of the "pastor's" hearing—and then the two would interact in front of all the trainees and supervisors. They would then be critiqued by all present. Those sessions were awkward, sometimes insightful, sometimes brutal.

One of the most difficult supervisors was a woman I'll call "Gracie." Her analysis of the role-playing was often quite caustic, and there was a bitter edge in it that seemed to go far beyond what was necessary or appropriate as critique.

2

Gracie was 33, had been blinded at age 12, and had suffered severe and debilitating rheumatoid arthritis for 30 years. Her feet and hands were swollen and malformed from it, and she shuffled slowly and painfully to walk. We all feared her criticisms, but I think all of us also felt sorry enough for her that no one ever objected to her razor-like words.

I came in for our group role-playing session one week and realized I had been "set up." There were probably 30 people in the room (supervisors and trainees). Gracie was asked to leave. I was given a marking pen and sent to the whiteboard, and the head of the program said, "You're the chaplain. Gracie will be your patient when she returns [with whatever disease they'd told her to pretend she had]. Prove to us before she comes back that God heals disease."

I wasn't sure what they expected me to do on the whiteboard to prove God heals. Scripture? History? Theology? My head was spinning, and I really didn't know what to do. Finally, I put the marker down and said, "I can't prove it. I haven't even seen it, though I have a good friend who has, and I trust his testimony."

This was not well-received, but they went on to phase two anyway. Gracie was invited back in and led to me. She came very close to my face. I saw she was weeping. She whispered to me, "I can't pretend. I have to do this for real." I said "me too," and we sat down in two chairs at right angles in the middle of the room, surrounded by all the others, who were watching us.

We held hands, closed our eyes, and I began to pray. Mind you, I had no clue how to do this. I could not have been more inexperienced, naïve or nervous. I don't even remember what I prayed, only that Gracie and I were willing to put ourselves before God for her healing.

Suddenly we were not in the room any longer. We were in what seemed like deep space, just the two of us, with the Holy Spirit. And though I understand theology says the Holy Spirit is a person, it was more like we were in the midst of God. Surrounded. Enfolded. It was safe there, and powerful, but we weren't nervous. I asked for Gracie to be healed. I have no idea how much time passed in this place.

Suddenly we were back in the room again. Someone's touch had surprised us and brought us back. Both Gracie and I were weeping, our noses running like crazy—we hadn't realized it—and one of the people, seeing this, was giving us tissues. I looked around, and everyone in the room was weeping loudly, and the presence of the Spirit of God was there in great weight and power. I'd never experienced anything like it.

We blew our noses, dried our eyes, and then held hands again. Instantly, we were no longer in the room but back in deep space with God. Next I heard myself being told that the reason for Gracie's rheumatoid arthritis was her father—that he had also had it, that she loved him and as a young child had "taken" it from him onto herself.

This seemed really *odd* to me (more about that later), and I knew nothing about her father. So I asked her, "Did your father have rheumatoid arthritis?" She said yes, since before she was born. She had come down with it at age three. I said something like, "You took it unto yourself because you loved him so much and wanted to take away his pain."

She made a small cry of recognition and said, "Yes." Then I looked up (eyes still closed, still in deep space) and saw purple irises. Nothing else, just purple irises. This also seemed quite odd to me, only this time I said nothing.

We let go of each other's hands, opened our eyes, and we were back in the room. No one moved or spoke. It was thick with the presence of God. We wiped our eyes again, and after a few minutes, everyone left quietly.

I had no idea what to make of the experience, no idea if any healing took place (Gracie looked the same), and I was wrapped in a silent peace. I headed home.

I had no further training that week, and I spoke to no one from the group until the following week. I called the training office to check on something, and the supervisor I reached said, "Did you hear what happened to Gracie?"

"No, what?" I had a sudden flush of anxiety. I worried that she had gotten ill, or died, and all because I had prayed with her, and now not only was healing prayer going to seem like a really awful idea, but I was responsible for harming Gracie.

"She's healed."

"What? *Healed?*" I was stunned.

"She's still blind. But the arthritis is completely gone. She's been to her doctors, and they told her that her sedimentation rate is absolutely normal. The pain is gone. She's walking like a normal person now. Gracie is healed. Now she comes in *singing* to work in the morning. She's happy. She bubbles. She's a completely different person. Everyone's talking about it."

I suppose I should have felt vindicated, or jumped and shouted "hallelujah" and "praise God," but my first reaction was simply relief: *I hadn't killed her!* It sounds silly, but that was my first thought.

The rest of the day I spent reeling from the news, still trying to comprehend what had happened, and I pondered the reality of it all deeply. Even though I had "believed" that God healed, this was a real shift in my understanding of *everything*. God changed "reality."

Then I remembered the purple irises.

I had no idea what they meant, and I hadn't said anything about seeing them to anyone. But somehow I knew what to do. Over the next few days I had a small card made in Braille, addressed to Gracie from me: "I saw these when we prayed." I bought purple irises at a florist, had them boxed with the card, and had them delivered.

The next afternoon, the phone rang at my desk. When I answered, an incredibly sweet, soft voice said, "Thank you for the flowers." I wasn't sure who it was. I thought it might be her, but the voice was unlike anything I'd ever heard come out of her mouth. I said incredulously, "Gracie?"

"Yes," she said. She invited me to lunch to share what had happened since we prayed. And then she said, "You can't have known this, but purple irises are my favorite flower in the whole world. I have a painting of them above my bed (even though she was blind). I wake up in that bed every morning now, praising God for my healing. Because the pain was so great, it used to take me two hours to get out of bed, clean up and get ready for work. Now it takes me fifteen minutes. My life is completely changed. And the purple irises you sent—another confirmation to me that He is real and **He knows me**."

We met a week or so later for lunch, laughing and sharing about God's goodness and our joy. Her primary ministry, she said, was counseling women who had been abused. She said that until her healing, she believed God was great and "awe-full" (her word), and this was the description of God she always shared with those she counseled. "But now," she said, "I know that He is *sweet*. I *know* it, and I tell them *they can know it too*."

I still own a small silver container Gracie gave me for healing oil, and the memory of this journey together with her into the presence of God continues to sustain me and bring me joy—as well as inform my understanding of God's sweetness and willingness to heal. He *knows* each of us.

SCRIPTURE, HISTORY AND THEOLOGY

Testimonies like the one just above are water for parched souls, and they embolden us to seek God for presence and healing. It was a trusted friend's testimony of a healing of severe scoliosis (I'll tell his story later) that gave me the courage (or foolishness) to pray with Gracie.

I want us to hold on to the precious work God did here, and in the many testimonies you will read in this book or hear about elsewhere in the years ahead. But I also want us to spend some important time unpacking what happened, and then also looking at the Scripture, history and theology that relate directly to this aspect of God's presence with us—those things my supervisors apparently wanted from me at the whiteboard but that I had no clue how to provide. In fact, this whole book will be given over to Scripture, history and theology, plus testimonies and *practical methods* in healing.

Let's be clear: God can and will heal when we pray, even if we don't have a clue how to explain, defend or prove that He is willing. But there is benefit in growing in our knowledge of the witness of Scripture, the theology that explains such things, and the history of God's interventions. We will draw from these, as well as testimonies of His healings, in order to set forth the "how to do it," or practical methods of actually *doing* healing prayer.

A friend might call and say "come on over to my house," and even if you'd never been, you might set out in the general direction and eventually find your way there. But it would be a great benefit if he gave you practical directions, told you which routes were the best, and advised "what to avoid" of muddy ravines, robbers and hornets' nests.

Scripture, history and theology will provide those directions, and will be quite practical for us. They are not unneeded extras, nor mere "theory," but valuable gifts for the traveler on this journey to God's healing presence.

Unpacking Gracie's Healing

It's been many years since Gracie's healing—years of being mentored, trying, failing, learning and unlearning—as I pressed in to understand more about how God healed, and to apply it to my life, prayer and ministry. This has given me some perspective on what happened on that day so many years ago. I can look back and see now what was opaque to me then.

The first and most-obvious insight about that day was that God did not require me to be an expert in healing prayer for my prayer to be effective. I'm not disparaging learning more about how to pray—this whole book is dedicated to that—but I want to be clear that God moves when He chooses, not because we structure our prayers just right.

More, He responds to willing hearts that come before Him trustingly, even if they are unsure, nervous, naïve, and don't even know quite how to begin. This was true of both Gracie and me. We were willing to let Him have His way with us.

Of course, there is the opposite as well—to pridefully jump into prayer not believing one needs any preparation or instruction—*refusing* to learn more about the nature and process of prayer. To proceed *that* way means that you will indeed find the hornets' nests. I have seen this happen when pride gets in the way.

The second insight is that God will come in power, and when He does so, even strong doubt is undone. It was a room full of people who did not believe in the supernatural (even though they were Christians training for ministry), who didn't believe God could intervene and change reality, and who doubted His living presence. But *when He came*, they *believed*. And it wasn't just an intellectual assent to a different theology about the modern-day activity of the Holy Spirit.[1] It was a life-changing moment for 30 doubters, because two people hungry for His power simply came before Him and asked.

I was told later by two of those present that they attended a party a couple weeks later with seminary students, some of whom began

---

[1] Some "cessationist" churches teach that this kind of miraculous activity ceased when the last apostle died.

making disparaging remarks about Christians who believed in miracles. Normally these two would have joined in the put-downs. But this time they exclaimed, "No. Wait. It's really true. We've seen it." They caused quite a stir. They had witnessed the power of God and would not shut up about it.

The third insight is that God knows things we don't, and He sometimes reveals them to us when we pray. I knew nothing of Gracie's father or his arthritis, and had someone told me she had "taken it from him" because she loved him, I'd have dismissed it as bad theology, bad psychology, and really bad science. And I could theorize as well as the next person about the "placebo effect" of suggesting to her that this was the cause of her disease and letting go of it could heal her. But that's just a giant supposition, years later, about a profound, supernatural healing that defies rational explanation. The Holy Spirit was there. *That's* why it happened.

My inexperience led me to simply say aloud what I had heard the Spirit say about Gracie's love for her father. The Spirit gave her the discernment to recognize the truth of it. And the Spirit healed her. Odd as it was, I was too nervous—and too moved by the Presence—to hedge my bets, protect my reputation (hah), and not say anything so ridiculous. I spoke what the Spirit said, she heard what the Spirit said, and she was healed by the Spirit.

A fourth insight is that the healing did not happen at that very instant. I don't know when the pain left and the swelling went down. I don't know when the sedimentation rate dropped back to normal. I don't know when the joy and sweetness came, except that it was not immediate. It came, though. It came.

A fifth insight came with the purple irises. As odd and unknowable as the "word of knowledge" (more on that later) was about her father, even odder and less likely was the vision of the irises. I had no way to know Gracie loved them, certainly no way to know she had a painting of them above her bed, and frankly found the vision so weird I said nothing about it at all until after her healing—when I knew it was time to take God's revelations far more seriously.

And more: When Gracie received the purple irises, knowing I had no human way of knowing of her love for them, it was a further deepening of her own faith in a sweet and loving God.

You might think, "That's all well and good, and perhaps God really is willing to heal people, but I just don't know enough about Him or His ways to really be effective. Isn't that what ministers, or evangelists, or saints are for?"

The short answer is: No. That's what *you* are for.

We will learn more of all of this as the pages ahead unfold, but take away at least this for now: *There is a God, and He is willing to heal. Just go willingly into His presence.*

It is your turn.

So, let's look at the Scriptures to begin to understand God's heart, and His leading for you, as the nature of healing begins to be revealed.

We'll start with the first part of Psalm 139, a song written by King David; the last part (not printed here) is valuable as well, as David rails against the enemies of God and asks that his own heart be searched. But for our initial purposes we will look at the first eighteen verses:

The God Who Knows Me

You have searched me, LORD, and you know me.
You know when I sit and when I rise;
you perceive my thoughts from afar.
You discern my going out and my lying down;
you are familiar with all my ways.
Before a word is on my tongue you, LORD,
know it completely.
You hem me in behind and before,
and you lay your hand upon me.
Such knowledge is too wonderful for me,
too lofty for me to attain.
Where can I go from your Spirit?
Where can I flee from your presence?
If I go up to the heavens, you are there;
if I make my bed in the depths, you are there.
If I rise on the wings of the dawn,
if I settle on the far side of the sea,
even there your hand will guide me,
your right hand will hold me fast.
If I say, "Surely the darkness will hide me
and the light become night around me,"
even the darkness will not be dark to you;
the night will shine like the day,
for darkness is as light to you.
For you created my inmost being;
you knit me together in my mother's womb.
I praise you because I am fearfully and wonderfully made;
your works are wonderful, I know that full well.
My frame was not hidden from you
when I was made in the secret place,
when I was woven together in the depths of the earth.[2]
Your eyes saw my unformed body;
all the days ordained for me were written in your book
before one of them came to be.
How precious to me are your thoughts, God.
How vast is the sum of them.
Were I to count them,
they would outnumber the grains of sand—
when I awake, I am still with you.[3]

---

[2] Interestingly, the English word "man" likely comes from a Sanskrit word meaning *the thinker made from the earth*, and the Hebrew word "Adam" means *made from earth*. See Genesis 2:7.
[3] Psalm 139:1–18, NIV.

This is such an extraordinary psalm that I hardly know where to begin. It contains deep wisdom and understanding of who God is, and what He knows, and how intimately He knows us, cares for us, and guides us. He knows everything about us—every thought, every need, every fear. He should be as precious to us as we are to Him, and though we sleep and are unaware of Him, when we wake up He is still right there. In fact, "the one who watches over you will not slumber."[4]

He never leaves. He watches all night long until you awake.

This should be obvious, but so many of us today—even Christians—act as if God created the world and left it on its own. At the most, we think He visited a few times in the past, and *maybe* comes occasionally into our lives or the lives of others. We are "functional Deists." We act like He doesn't know our needs and really doesn't much care. We don't think of Him as being intimate with us, like a loving spouse, never leaving our side, looking lovingly at us all night long. Yet such an intimate, caring and jealous God is what Scripture reveals.

THE GOD WHO SPEAKS

Aside from people whose disabilities prevent it, can you imagine a marriage in which the husband and wife never speak (all kidding aside)? Rather, those marriages that are healthiest are intimate not just in physical closeness, but in words whispered in love, in plans made together, in warnings given in times of danger, in instruction where it is needed, in talking out loud.

The Apostle Paul, writing to Christian believers, reminded them of how different the real God is from the idols they once worshiped:

> Now, dear brothers and sisters, regarding your question about the special abilities the Spirit gives us. I don't want you to misunderstand this. You know that when you were still pagans, you were led astray and swept along in worshiping speechless idols. So I want you to know that no one speaking by the Spirit of God will curse Jesus, and no one can say Jesus is Lord, except by the Holy Spirit.[5]

We'll return to this passage later. For now, notice this key insight: The idols they once worshiped were silent. And maybe more pointedly, it wasn't that they refused to speak; they just plain couldn't. They were carved wood, or clay, or stone. Speechless, of course.

---

[4] Psalm 121:3b.
[5] 1 Corinthians 12:1–2.

Paul intends the obvious implication: GOD SPEAKS TO US. This may happen in a thousand different ways, from actual audible words, to Scripture, dreams, visions, angels, convictions of the heart, worship, prayer, and especially *through other believers, led by the Spirit of God to speak to us from God's heart.* This is why Paul says, "No one speaking by the Spirit of God will curse Jesus, and no one can say Jesus is Lord, except by the Holy Spirit." Paul is speaking of the quality and content of believers when their speech is from God—speaking by the Spirit of God—as *God speaks to us* through them.

One of God's prophets, Elijah, was fleeing from Jezebel, who had vowed to kill him:

> Elijah was afraid and fled for his life. He went to Beersheba, a town in Judah, and he left his servant there. Then he went on alone into the wilderness, traveling all day. He sat down under a solitary broom tree and prayed that he might die. "I have had enough, LORD," he said.
>
> "Take my life, for I am no better than my ancestors who have already died."
>
> Then he lay down and slept under the broom tree. But as he was sleeping, an angel touched him and told him, "Get up and eat." He looked around and there beside his head was some bread baked on hot stones and a jar of water. So he ate and drank and lay down again.
>
> Then the angel of the LORD came again and touched him and said, "Get up and eat some more, or the journey ahead will be too much for you."
>
> So he got up and ate and drank, and the food gave him enough strength to travel forty days and forty nights to Mount Sinai, the mountain of God. There he came to a cave, where he spent the night.
>
> But the LORD said to him, "What are you doing here, Elijah?"
>
> Elijah replied, "I have zealously served the LORD God Almighty. But the people of Israel have broken their covenant with you, torn down your altars, and killed every one of your prophets. I am the only one left, and now they are trying to kill me, too."
>
> "Go out and stand before me on the mountain," the LORD told him. And as Elijah stood there, the LORD passed by, and a mighty windstorm hit the mountain. It was such a terrible blast that the rocks were torn loose, but the LORD was not in the wind. After the wind there was an earthquake, but the LORD was not in the earthquake. And after the earthquake there was a fire, but the LORD was not in the fire. And after the fire there was *the sound of a gentle whisper.* When Elijah heard it, he wrapped his face in his cloak and went out and stood at the entrance of the cave.
>
> And a voice said, "What are you doing here, Elijah?"[6]

---

[6] 1 Kings 19:3–13.

God spoke to Adam and Eve, to Noah, Hagar, Abram, Isaac, Jacob, Moses, Aaron, Balaam, Deborah, Eli, Samuel, David, Solomon, Ahijah, Jeroboam, Elijah, Elisha, Nathan, Gad, Shemaiah, Zechariah, Huldah, Isaiah, Jeremiah, Ezekiel, Daniel, Mary, Joseph, Jesus, the Wise Men, Peter, John, Saul/Paul, Ananias...[7]

We often think of prayer as *us speaking to God*, but it's not a one-way channel. It is a *conversation*, if we will open ourselves to listen to Him.

> The boy Samuel ministered before the LORD under Eli. In those days the word of the LORD was rare; there were not many visions. One night Eli, whose eyes were becoming so weak that he could barely see, was lying down in his usual place. The lamp of God had not yet gone out, and Samuel was lying down in the house of the LORD, where the ark of God was. Then the LORD called Samuel.
>
> Samuel answered, "Here I am." And he ran to Eli and said, "Here I am; you called me."
>
> But Eli said, "I did not call; go back and lie down." So he went and lay down.
>
> Again the LORD called, "Samuel." And Samuel got up and went to Eli and said, "Here I am; you called me."
>
> "My son," Eli said, "I did not call; go back and lie down."
>
> Now Samuel did not yet know the LORD: The word of the LORD had not yet been revealed to him.
>
> A third time the LORD called, "Samuel." And Samuel got up and went to Eli and said, "Here I am; you called me."
>
> Then Eli realized that the LORD was calling the boy. So Eli told Samuel, "Go and lie down, and if he calls you, say, 'Speak, LORD, for your servant is listening.'" So Samuel went and lay down in his place.
>
> The LORD came and stood there, calling as at the other times, "Samuel. Samuel."
>
> Then Samuel said, "Speak, for your servant is listening."[8]

The testimony of Gracie's healing is an example of this. I both heard a word from the Lord about her father's arthritis, and I saw purple irises. These are but two examples of how God speaks (I mentioned a few others just above), and they are *every bit as much available to you* as they are to me. In the chapters ahead we'll look more deeply at the nature of this conversation with God, and the various "gifts" that are the

---

[7] Often directly—through angels, people, and other ways beyond words.
[8] 1 Samuel 3:1–10.

13

hallmark of a relationship with Him, but for now just realize that this is intended to be *normative* for followers of Jesus.[9]

We have a God who speaks. And we can *learn* how to listen. Real healing comes from the real God.

---

[9] Or *Yeshua.* See Appendix C for a brief, helpful discussion of His name.

2.
The Victims of Sin

The world is filled with victims. This includes those who are victims of disease, accident, abuse, oppression, physical, mental and emotional violence, injury, war, slavery, sex trafficking, and more, and also—to be blunt—those who are either stuck or *acting* in a daily role of victimhood. Healing is available for *all* of these conditions, and this book will reveal Who does it and how *you* can be a part of it. First, some foundational insights.

THE PROBLEM

Sin and the redemption of the sinner are the focus of much of the Church's theology as well as the fuel of its strivings to save the world. The Church uses both fear of judgment and invitation to a better life to help individuals turn from their lives of sin to Jesus as the way of salvation. While this is an essential part of the Good News of Jesus Christ, *it is not all of it.*

Sin is not victimless, but the Church often seems devoted primarily to the redemption of *sinners* and only secondarily to the victims of sin. Yet the Gospel is also for the *victims* of sin, and it promises redemption and *healing* for them.

Romans 5:9 is usually translated, "Having now been justified by His blood, we shall be saved from wrath through Him." The *New Living Translation*: "He will certainly save us from God's judgment." Explanations of this verse usually emphasize how we are under God's judgment because of our sin and how we can be 'acquitted' because Jesus, who was innocent, took our place. In this theology, some assert that God is justifiably angry toward us but that we escape His wrath because of Jesus. But it would be truer to the original text to say that God's wrath[10] is against *evil*. We are subject to His wrath because as sinners we are participants in evil, immersed in evil, literally "devoted to sin, evil."[11] Romans 5:8 declares, "God demonstrates His own love toward us, in that while we were still sinners [still devoted to evil], Christ died for us."

This verse illuminates what the Gospel is about. God is angry about evil but loves us so much that Christ died for us even while we were still devoted to evil. That's what the text says. So let's dig deeper.

---

10 Wrath: ὀργῆς (*orgēs*).
11 Evil: ἁμαρτωλῶν (*hamartōlōn*).

WHY IS GOD ANGRY ABOUT EVIL?

This is a foundational question. Is it because it interferes with His will? Because Satan is competition for Him? If so, God is petty and insecure and, thus, not God. Rather, He is angry about evil because of the harm it does, because of the relationships it destroys, and because of the suffering it causes—in short, *because it has victims.*

There is no victimless sin. For every sinner and sin there is *always* a victim. Sometimes the victims are the sinners themselves; more often the victims are others. But there are always victims, and Jesus died for them too. There isn't anyone He **didn't** die for. His heart clearly was for the marginalized, the poor, the outcast, the prisoners, the blind and the wounded. He even told us that when we served *them*, we served *Him*:

> Assuredly, I say to you, inasmuch as you did it to one of the least of these My brethren, you did it to Me.[12]

The world and the Church are filled with sinners, but they are also full of sin's victims. And just as Jesus desired to heal both sinners and the sinned against while He walked on earth, He wants us, as His body, to serve and heal them both in the world today. He loved and touched and healed them, and He commanded us to do the same. "Heal" is both the command Jesus gave to those He healed, and the command He gave His followers when He sent them into the world. It is the command He gives us, you and me.

The Good News is for *both* the *redemption of sinners* (all of us) and the *healing of the sinned against* (also all of us). Without both of these, the Gospel is incomplete.

Sin wounds—physically, mentally, emotionally, spiritually. That is why God hates it and why He loves to heal its victims. And just as there are great sinners (i.e., those whose devotion to evil has many victims), so are there great victims (i.e., those who have been crippled by the great sin done to them).

The Church must be willing to see and offer the Good News to both, yet it often ignores or marginalizes the victims while it attends to and redeems the victimizers.

---

[12] Matthew 25:40.

Healing prayer is focused on healing victims from the effects of sin. This must apply to all, and most certainly it must include those most profoundly wounded.

SPECIAL TERMS

A few of the terms in this book are used in a special way and require explicit definition. Those whose meanings may be unique or uncommon include:

- **Healing Prayer:** Prayer that explicitly seeks and relies upon God's supernatural intervention through the agency of the Holy Spirit for the healing of victims of sin in the physical, mental, emotional and spiritual dimensions of their lives.
- **Woeful:** a category referring to the sinned against, their state of victimization and oppression, their **Woe**, and the consequences of sin on them, whether caused by an individual or an institution.
- **Peculiar:** A term used colloquially to describe people who are social misfits, often as a result of their woundedness as victims of sin. Ironically, in older English usage, "peculiar" meant "a hidden treasure." See Deut. 14:2 and 1 Peter 2:9, KJV.

This book, *Healing Prayer*, rests on the biblical revelation that God can and does heal. In the Old Testament, one of the names God uses to identify himself is יהוה רפאך—*Yehovah Rapha*—"the LORD who heals you."[13]

Psalm 103:1–3 is also relevant: "Bless the LORD, O my soul; and all that is within me, bless His holy name. Bless the LORD, O my soul, and forget not all His benefits: Who forgives all your iniquities, Who heals all your diseases." Some say that God is a forgiver but not a healer. Such people are WRONG.

Healing has occurred throughout the history of the Church, even though at times it is has faded among those who disbelieved, failed to ask, or injected misunderstandings and theological error into their concept of God. This book relies upon God's numerous promises in Scripture to heal, His healing initiatives throughout history, and the belief that healing can be *taught* and *"caught."* Since healing can be demonstrated, experienced, and learned by others, the effectiveness and the success of the teaching can also be *seen*.

---

[13] See Exodus 15:26. רָפָא (*rapha*) means "to heal."

SINNERS NEED FORGIVENESS.
SIN'S VICTIMS NEED HEALING.

Healing, as construed in this book, is confined to repair and recovery from wounding. It is distinguished from forgiveness and redemption from sin, which are used here to refer to sinners who victimize. Broader definitions of these terms might allow them to cover both kinds of needs—of sinner and sinned against—but they are used narrowly here for the sake of clarity.

Jesus sent His disciples, empowered by the Holy Spirit, into the entire world to share the Good News and to heal and minister much as He did.

Some victims of sin have overcome their wounding; others can seem quite "normal" and not attract attention. But still others often have physical or social "affects" that single them out for ostracism or belittling. Our culture (including the Church) views many of them as "peculiar," and many in the Church at large are uneasy at their presence or behavior, such as self-destructiveness, substance misuse, weight gain or loss, withdrawal, sexual confusion, helplessness, or other disability. Some dress oddly, are unclean, or act in other ways outside social norms.

So wounded are these people that often they believe, *I deserve the scorn I experience.* They see themselves as unworthy of respect or love, whether from other people or from God. At times the wounding causes them to invent a new persona in an attempt to escape the pain, and to disguise the one who was in harm's way. This can even appear to result in multiple persona (called "parts" or "alters") in a single person, who presents to the world the one that seems appropriate in the face of a specific need or threat.[14]

Of course, some victims of sin can appear quite "normal." They manage to develop or maintain a normal affect and thus appear without obvious wounds. But the sin of which they are victims still intrudes into their lives and disables them, leaving them broken and incomplete, just in less-obvious ways—some hidden and some delayed in time, to burst forth later in life.

Clearly, training in healing must acknowledge a vast range of needs in those being prayed for, and this book teaches those who pray for healing to be sensitive to these realities, to avoid judging on appearances, and to withhold the kind of disdain common in our culture and in our churches. Nevertheless, the practical essentials of

---

[14] James Friesen, *Uncovering the Mystery of MPD* [Multiple Personality Disorder], 41–67.

healing prayer can be taught regardless of the specific need or the depth of the wounding.

Understanding how to willingly seek God's intervention, how to give up control to the Holy Spirit, and how not to interfere or misdirect are the basic elements of healing prayer, and they are independent of the degree of need. They are not just for the profoundly wounded or their wounds, though these are important. Teaching about the badly victimized is an element of the overall training, but not its sole focus. Understanding deep need equips those who pray to respond more broadly to all needs, but the basic elements remain the same across the spectrum.

The effects and affects described here are common consequences of sin, and as such, they are open to healing through prayer. Professional therapy and medicine (including psychiatry) can also be effective in a victim's recovery, but those who pray who are not trained in these fields must avoid amateur attempts at these professions. Professionals (doctors, counselors, etc.) can of course learn healing prayer, and it can prove of great value in their work. But the temptation for non-professionals to engage in medicine or psychology must be strictly avoided. If you are not a professional, don't try to be.

Jesus charged His disciples to heal the sick, and we are the inheritors of this charge. Just as Jesus trained His disciples by "use and practice" (one of the root meanings of *disciple* in Greek), those who have learned healing prayer teach it by doing, by explaining what is being done, and by inviting those being discipled *to do it as well*.

When we (that is, disciples) pray, the Holy Spirit responds willingly with healing. Even in large group trainings, it is not uncommon to see the Holy Spirit touch and heal people profoundly throughout a room, even though the prayer is apparently focused on just the person in front. When invited, the Spirit "blows where it wishes" (John 3:8), which is often well beyond even the trainers' expectations. It is eloquent testimony to God's willingness to heal. Jesus explained this willingness:

> For everyone who asks receives, and he who seeks finds, and to him who knocks it will be opened. If a son asks for bread from any father among you, will he give him a stone? Or if he asks for a fish, will he give him a serpent instead of a fish? Or if he asks for an egg, will he offer him a scorpion? If you then, being evil, know how to give good gifts to your

children, how much more will your heavenly Father give the Holy Spirit to those who ask Him.[15]

In teaching believers to exercise this gift of healing, it must be made clear that this promise of Jesus is not a spiritual abstraction but a real event with a real effect in the real physical world. Hold on to this: If anything, God CAN heal (if He chooses) and often DOES (but it's not a guarantee)—and for that matter, if He IS going to heal, He can do it through absolutely anyone He wants—"expert" or not. Including you and me.

In some cases, the coming of the Holy Spirit produces *physical* healing. In others, it frees people from the destructive intrusion of the past into their *minds, emotions* and *spirit*. That is, instead of being disabled by the wounding and damage of the past, they are released from its power and begin new chapters in their lives, free from the bondage that was their constant reality. In time, they often become the most compassionate and willing to pray for the healing of others.

The Holy Spirit directs and empowers this change through healing prayer—prayer that directly seeks the Spirit's intervention in people's lives for the healing of the effects of the sins committed against them by others and by themselves, as well as for their ongoing growth, discipling, healing and sanctification.

Thus, the basic assumptions of healing prayer are:
- Victims of sin, injury and disease need healing.
- Healing is repair and recovery from wounding, not forgiveness from sin.[16]
- Through the Holy Spirit, Jesus empowered His followers to be healers.

With this foundation laid, the message of this book is clear: *By the power of the Holy Spirit, victims of sin, injury and disease can be healed, and believers in the Body of Christ can be trained to be the agents of this healing.*

Of course, these victims are not just the badly wounded, nor are most of the elements of healing prayer specific to the needs only of the most wounded. The foundational aspects of healing prayer are broadly applicable.

---

[15] Luke 11:10–13.
[16] More on this to come in the pages and chapters ahead.

All of us are sinners (including those badly sinned against), and the ministry of healing prayer does not seek to minimize or ignore this. In fact, healing the damage of sin done to us sometimes begins with our receiving forgiveness for the damage we ourselves have caused. But often this is not true, and healing for the victims of sin has specific characteristics, dimensions and requirements that are often unknown or ignored by the Church. Perhaps this is why the profoundly wounded are more likely to seek out opportunities for healing prayer, or attend teaching on the subject, than those who are less obviously wounded.

In healing prayer, the Holy Spirit is invited to work in the prayer ministers and in the victim, both to lead to forgiveness of others and to the healing of the damage done to the victim. This prayer is appropriate for anyone, since all are sinned against, just as all are sinners, but it brings particular satisfaction and joy when those who have been badly hurt are healed. As the healing unfolds, even the people once regarded as peculiar by an often-cruel culture and church are revealed to be God's "peculiar" people in the sense intended by the King James Bible, which uses *peculiar* to translate the Hebrew word meaning "treasure," "jewel" or "valued property":

Thou art a holy people unto the Lord thy God, and the Lord hath chosen thee to be a peculiar[17] people unto himself, above all the nations that are upon the earth.[18]

BACKGROUND AND SIGNIFICANCE

There are a significant number of healing ministries in the Church at large today, ranging from charlatanry to genuine, caring, and effective efforts, but even in the best of these, there is little other than the healing itself. That sounds odd to say—since healing is wonderful—but the secret of God's gifts to us is that *they are used to bless others*. Those who are healed should learn to do healing prayer themselves.

Perhaps combining the best lessons from these healings with insights from Scripture and the leading of the Holy Spirit can produce a resource that will benefit the individuals being trained and allow them to take the training home to impact the world at large.

This is particularly important to the Church in its understanding and care of "peculiar" people. Not all who seek healing prayer have so profound and apparent a wounding as these. While some people come

---

[17] סְגֻלָּה (*segullah*). Hebrew for "treasure," "jewel," "valued property."
[18] Deuteronomy 14:2, KJV.

for healing prayer much as they would visit the family doctor for a minor illness, the ministry of healing prayer would be a failure if it served only such needs.

It is in its ability to serve those more seriously wounded that the Church gains true understanding about the depths of God's love and His willingness to heal.

Because many in the Church have not even thought about the badly sinned against, much less learned how to love and heal them, these people quickly realize that they do not fit and are not understood, and they therefore feel pain while in church and quickly flee. This is both an acknowledgment of how the Church has failed to be Christ's Body and a challenge to it to grow in Christlikeness.

I have delighted in how powerfully the Holy Spirit moves when invited, and how touched people are who have witnessed His power, experienced His infilling, or been healed by Him. The ministry of healing prayer is very focused on how these transformational experiences have the power to draw unbelievers to Jesus Christ and believers into a deeper healing and sanctifying relationship with God through the Holy Spirit.

Healing is always a sovereign move of God, not something that can be forced, packaged or manufactured. Yet there are areas where training is important:

- In correcting misunderstandings about the nature of healing.
- In identifying things that can act as barriers and distractions.
- In finding methods to focus participants and lead to greater effectiveness in prayer.

Some churches put little emphasis on the Holy Spirit, and "cessationists" believe that the miraculous healing work of the Holy Spirit ceased after the Apostolic Age. While the principles of healing prayer are broadly applicable, some additional teaching and caution may be required in introducing this teaching in such venues.

3.
Sin, Sin, Sin

SIN AND THE SINNED AGAINST

To understand the work of the Holy Spirit in healing prayer, we must grasp the nature of sin and its transmission. There is a profound, destructive relationship between the sinner and the sinned against. Study of and commentary on relevant Scriptures is needed to understand the roles of salvation, sanctification, confession, forgiveness and healing for the sinner and the sinned against. The passages in this chapter represent and are foundational to the theology and practice of healing prayer. They are meant to clarify its nature and scope, grounding us in the theological conviction that healing prayer touches both sides of the problem of sin, but focuses primarily on the sinned against.

During their wandering in the wilderness, the Israelites rebelled against God time and again. At Kadesh-Barnea, God was about to destroy them for their numerous sins, but Moses reminded Him of what He had said about His judgment and mercy:

> And now, I pray, let the power of my Lord be great, just as You have spoken, saying, "The LORD is longsuffering and abundant in mercy, forgiving iniquity and transgression; but He by no means clears the guilty, visiting the iniquity of the fathers on the children to the third and fourth generation." Pardon the iniquity of this people, I pray, according to the greatness of Your mercy, just as You have forgiven this people, from Egypt even until now.
>
> Then the LORD said: "I have pardoned, according to your word; but truly, as I live, all the earth shall be filled with the glory of the LORD—because all these men who have seen My glory and the signs which I did in Egypt and in the wilderness, and have put Me to the test now these ten times, and have not heeded My voice, they certainly shall not see the land of which I swore to their fathers, nor shall any of those who rejected Me see it." (Numbers 14:17–23)

At Moses' plea, God withdrew the death sentence, but the physical consequences and the lesson of the Israelites' sin persisted: They would not see the Promised Land. The translation of "visiting the iniquity" in this passage is consistent with much of Hebrew thought, which holds that God, being sovereign and omnipotent, is responsible for everything, including the evil we experience. This is not to say that He is the author of evil, but that everything, for it to happen at all, must be within His "permissive" will; He allows it. Therefore, "visiting the iniquity," or punishing future generations for the sins of their parents, would not mean that God unjustly intended the harm, but that it could only occur because He allowed it to.

This view is expressed often in Hebrew Scripture, and many Christian theologians agree with it. For example, regarding Romans 8:20 ("For the creature was made subject to vanity, not willingly, but by reason of him who hath subjected the same in hope...", John Wesley wrote, "The creation was made subject to vanity—abuse, misery, and corruption. By him who subjected it—namely, God, *Genesis 3:17, 5:29*."[19] That is, God made creation, and us, subject to abuse, misery and corruption.

This idea is often difficult for modern readers to grasp. They read this and ask, "Why is God so mean that He punishes children for the sins their parents commit?"

A historical parallel can help account for this difference in thought. In ancient times, people believed God or His angels pushed the stars and planets across the sky. The assumption was that if God stopped pushing, everything would stop. The modern view is that God established the laws of physics, and stars and planets alike obey those laws. When you throw a ball, it flies through the air because it has momentum—you only have to throw it once. Likewise, God set the planets and stars in motion—He doesn't have to repeatedly move them. Both the ancient and modern views attempt to explain what is observed, but whatever the explanation, the stars and planets still move. This can help us understand the passage from Numbers.

Consider the substrata of the Hebrew. The words for *visiting* (פָּקַד, *paqad*) and *iniquity* (עָוֹן, `*avon*) are important.[20] The first can mean not only to reckon or to punish, but also to witness or watch over. The second can mean not only fault or sin, but also the consequences of sin. So another way to say that God is "visiting the iniquity of the fathers on the children to the third and fourth generation" is to say that God *witnesses the consequences of sin* committed by one generation *as sin infects and flows through subsequent generations.*

---

[19] See https://ccel.org/ccel/wesley/notes/notes.i.vii.ix.html for Wesley's note on Romans 8, from *Wesley's Notes on the Bible*.
[20] The underlying Hebrew word translated *visiting* also has broader implications. It is God's presence that brings blessing or judgment, and even both at the same time.

24

This is clearly true in families and nations. Sin does not stop with its perpetrators. Not only does it harm its victims, but it also harms—and even leads into sin—those in its wake. It has a ripple effect in the networks of relationships surrounding the sinner and in the lives of children, grandchildren, and so on "to the third and fourth generation." Everyone has seen and experienced this truth, and whether it occurs because God makes it happen, or because He allows it, and witnesses it, and testifies to it, does not change the reality that it *does* happen. It might be more useful to simply realize that because people are created in God's image, they are made to be in relationship with one another, and thus the sins (and love and good deeds) of the individual always affect more than just that person. They affect the people the sinner touches, and the people they touch, and so on and so on.

This is an extraordinarily important insight because much of the theology and teaching in the Church (particularly the Western Church) has been focused on sinners and their need for repentance. This is a vital concern, to be sure, but of at least equal importance is the consequence of sin on its victims. Not only are they often crippled physically, emotionally or spiritually by the sin of the sinner, but they are also often drawn into sin—either the same one or another—in reaction to it.

Thus, the abused often become abusers, or, conversely, they express their wounding in many ways—such as through eating disorders, sexual promiscuity, self-injury, drug or alcohol abuse, or bitter, fearful or icy relationships with others and with God. The truth is that just as all are sinners, all are also *sinned against*. This can help us understand and empathize—to a degree—with even the greatest victims of sin and suffering.

SIN AND SINNERS

Most Western theology has focused on the redemption and restoration of sinners.[21] It says sin separates people from God, and no amount of "being good" can make them holy enough to live in His presence. But when they confess and accept His forgiveness, they are forgiven. God extends His grace to them on the basis of Jesus' sacrifice on the cross—His willingness to die as a sinner though He is Himself without sin (Philippians 2). Jesus is standing in for men and women so God can declare them righteous and set them free—a gift we need only accept. But this is not the end of the story.

---

[21] Earl Wilson, et al., *Restoring the Fallen*, 41–51.

God desires for His people to move beyond salvation into *sanctification*[22]— that they be healed and r*eformed* and *matured* into His likeness. For this, He gives them the Holy Spirit as their advocate, counselor, intercessor and sanctifier. After salvation, the Spirit, who worked in them to free them from slavery to sin, now works to progressively free them from sin's influence and its worldly consequences.

It is in this light that some theologians based their understanding of the expression "He came to set the captives free," which is based on Luke 4:18, where Jesus, reading Isaiah 61:1, says:

> The Spirit of the LORD is upon Me, because He has anointed Me to preach the gospel to the poor; He has sent Me to heal the brokenhearted, to proclaim liberty to the captives and recovery of sight to the blind, to set at liberty those who are oppressed.

Christ *did* come to *free sinners* from their sins and from the often-intolerable consequences of their sin. But this is not the meaning of the passage this saying is based on. The language of Luke 4:18, and of the original text in Isaiah 61:1, is focused not on sinners and freeing them from their sin, but on the *victims of sin and misery*.

Here Jesus is not a philosophical abstraction of humanity and divinity residing in one body, however theologically attractive that abstraction might be. Rather, here is Jesus, a *real* person who touches *real* people who are *really* ill, *really* suffering, and *really* oppressed—and He *heals them*.

When Christ came and took *everything* upon himself—sin, suffering, death itself—He was also showing us that there is no suffering, no pain, no torment that He Himself did not know (and thus *does* know). There's a dual takeaway: (1) Whatever we feel and suffer, He too experienced it; and (2)—in turn—there is nothing He did not defeat and nothing He cannot heal.[23]

He lives not in royal splendor befitting a God-man, but in the midst of the most wounded of society, and *right there* He reveals the very heart of the Father.[24]

---

[22] See my book *What We Believe and Why* for a thorough explanation of the differences of salvation, sanctification and glorification.

[23] And yes, we don't understand why some people do not receive the healing they ask for, but we do know that it is not because God somehow doesn't care about some people as much as others. He does not "withhold healing" as a means of punishment, but there are still mysteries that are beyond our understanding, and why some are not healed is one of those.

[24] Bryan Stone, *Compassionate Ministry: Theological Foundations*, 70.

4.
Healing Prayer

SIN AND HEALING PRAYER

Many theologians have attempted to understand sin in the context of God's foreknowledge and the concept of predestination. The works of Augustine, Scotus and Calvin are examples of this line of thought. Some recent theologians advocate a view of sinfulness in which God, by His own (self-limiting) choice, is without foreknowledge of our actions and thus moves and suffers with us as we sin or evolve.

Just as Calvin and others argued for the omniscience of God across eternity,[25] so the advocates of "openness" argue that a God who can change His mind or regret an action cannot know the future.[26] Both of these positions (and variations thereof) can lead to paralysis in healing prayer—the first because of the fear that everything is already determined anyway, and the second because God may be perceived as not able or willing to help.

This book acknowledges but will not attempt to critique or weigh the relative merit of these contrasting views. Not only are the details and areas of disagreement and debate substantial, they are also beyond the scope of this book. I mention them here only to help us avoid paralysis.

Thus the training here is substantially and intentionally much simpler: *Sin hurts people, and this has lasting consequences.* "Sin is not only an act of wrongdoing but a state of alienation from God. ... It signifies the rupture of a personal relationship with God, a betrayal of the trust He places in us."[27] According to this definition, *wrongdoing* and the *consequent alienation* from God are the essence of sin. The way it's "supposed to be" is life as God designed it: a holy, unfractured wholeness, with people in intimate communion with Him.

People are sinners because they commit wrongful acts, and these acts alienate them from God.

---

[25] See John Calvin, *Institutes of the Christian Religion.*
[26] As implied in, "Then God saw their works, that they turned from their evil way; and God relented from the disaster that He had said He would bring upon them, and He did not do it" (Jonah 3:10), and "The LORD was sorry that He had made man on the earth, and He was grieved in His heart" (Genesis 6:6), for example.
[27] Walter A. Elwell, *Evangelical Dictionary of Theology*, 1012.

While there may be sins that involve no physical action (e.g., Matt. 5:28: "I say to you that whoever looks at a woman to lust for her has already committed adultery with her in his heart"), the sins in view in this study are mainly those that involve the harm and exploitation of others and the consequences that flow from "evil acts [that] "violate *shalom*."[28] These consequences can be addressed through human acts (e.g., aid, counsel, medicine, *all of which* can be effective) and by seeking, through prayer, direct intervention from God. This understanding is accepted and testified to by those who minister healing prayer, and it is taught here.

SIN AND VICTIMS

There are two sides to sin: the *sinners* and the *sinned against*. All of us are both, sometimes even as the consequence of the same sin. Nevertheless, the Church must recognize that there are some, like murderers and rapists, who are egregious sinners, and others, like victims of rape, violence and abuse, or those oppressed by evil regimes, who are profoundly sinned against. For individuals who are *sinned against* the issues of confession, forgiveness, salvation and sanctification take on added dimensions and demand *serious* re-examination.

Jesus' ministry repeatedly testifies to this. The powerful, the self-righteous and those who cheated others were the targets of His anger, while the poor, weak and powerless—the suffering and oppressed— were the principal audience for His proclamation of the Good News and were the primary objects of His healing.[29]

We might give this state of suffering a meaningful label: *Woe*, and its subjects, the *Woeful*.[30] It refers to a state of oppression and victimization that is a consequence of sin against a person, whether the cause is an individual or an institution. *Woeful* also refers to those who suffer even in the absence of someone who has sinned against them, such as victims of a disease, accident or natural disaster. As a proper noun, *Woeful* refers

---

[28] Cornelius Plantinga, *Not the Way It's Supposed to Be: A Breviary of Sin*, 10.

[29] James Moore Hickson, *The Healing of Christ in His Church*, 17.

[30] Andrew Sung Park, *The Wounded Heart of God: The Asian Concept of Han and the Christian Doctrine of Sin*, 15–16. Park has helped the Church realize that in focusing primarily on the *sinner* and salvation, it often doesn't even see the *sinned against*. Park introduced the Korean term *Han* as a label for this category. I use the term *Woeful* instead. Helpfully, Park says: "There is hope at the very foundation of our existence. ... Hope is the window of the soul. That is, when we look out and look forward, we can exist. When it is frustrated, hope turns into han [woe], a psychosomatic pain. Han [woe] produces sadness, resentment, aggression, and helplessness. ... It is the hardened heart that is grieved by oppression and injustice. ... When people are betrayed by those they have trusted, they become hopeless and experience despair. Children who have been abused often mistrust their parents and fall into hopelessness and despair. This hopelessness is not sin but han [woe]."

to the victims of sin and other innocent sufferers.[31] It also is used to refer to victims who are the cause of, or are complicit in, their own suffering, such as addicts of many kinds. *Woeful* is a useful, single, short word for this broad category of sufferers.

Exodus provides an early and essential insight into the nature of *Woe* and the *Woeful*. After the Israelites moved into Egypt, the Egyptians, who had been saved from famine by Joseph's prophecy and wisdom, accepted them as neighbors, and the Israelites apparently enjoyed comfortable lives. But later a king arose in Egypt who did not remember Joseph, and he enslaved the Israelites and made their lives bitter and hard.

God was not punishing them, and they had done *nothing* to harm the Egyptians. Still, they were stripped of rights, oppressed, and abused. They became hopeless; they endured *Woe*; they became *Woeful*.

Their attitudes were sadly emblematic of many of the *Woeful:* They did not believe God would rescue them, and when Moses interceded for them with Pharaoh, they accused him of making their lives worse. They preferred to remain in *woe* rather than endure the travail needed to free them, though God had promised to prevail on their behalf. Even Moses, the one God called and equipped to lead them to freedom and abundance, was afraid of the Egyptian victimizers and considered himself incompetent to lead the Israelites.

If Sin is the state of the sinner, *Woe* is the state of the sinned against and those who suffer from any cause. There are Sinners, and there are the *Woeful*. Both need salvation and loving, healing ministry, *but the nature of the ministry to each is quite different*. Realizing this can deepen insights gained from Scripture and may even open up some passages that, like Numbers 14, seem opaque, confusing or troubling, particularly as Scripture seldom testifies to a causal connection between sin and the suffering of *disease*, though it often connects sin to its consequences.[32]

The truth that all people are both sinners and *woeful* does not excuse perpetrators' evil acts. It will not do to say, "I couldn't help myself. I'm a victim; I acted out of pain." When victimhood is real and deep, it ought be acknowledged, but it is not an excuse for people who don't want to face their own sinfulness. When people sin, they are culpable, and they need to be forthright in confessing it, whatever their circumstances.

---

[31] *Innocent* here does not mean "without sin"; it means "without culpability in this particular suffering."
[32] L. Gregory Jones, *Embodying Forgiveness: A Theological Analysis*, 197–204.

On the other hand, *the victims of sin should not be led to confess guilt or complicity* if it is not there. Nor should they be summarily dismissed because some people are unwilling to believe, for example, that an upstanding, educated adult would sexually abuse a child, even though that is often the case.[33] This is self-evidently true in the lives of those who were abused as children, but it is often true in other circumstances as well. It is *damaging* to the individual who was harmed, and to his or her understanding of God's justice, to say that they *must have been a willing participant* in a sin in which they were simply a victim.

Although all individuals are sinners and sinned against, victimizers and victims, they are not *both* in each *instance*. Abuse victims are *not complicit* in the sin done to them. Thus, the sinned against must neither be pushed to confess nor be condemned for something they did not cause. It exacerbates their suffering to do so.

Equally, the victimizers should not be excused because they claim victim status themselves.

Of course there are instances where adults have sinned with and against each other, and where one claims victimhood against the other in their dispute. And the complications of relationship, history, power, memory, deceit, invention, manipulation and blackmail often confuse and misdirect any help, counsel or prayer that might be offered. There are serious dangers here. Great caution and patience are needed.

Also consider this: Not all instances of harm are the result of someone's sin. Be cautious. Be discerning. Jesus demonstrated this in His encounter with a man born blind:

> Now as Jesus passed by, He saw a man who was blind from birth. And His disciples asked Him, saying, "Rabbi, who sinned, this man or his parents, that he was born blind?" Jesus answered, "Neither this man nor his parents sinned, but that the works of God should be revealed in him." (John 9:1–3)

Here Jesus says that this man's *woe*, his suffering, is not the result of anyone's sin. His blindness is his condition, and Jesus heals it, revealing the working of God through Jesus. This should be a chastening reminder to those who believe in karma and imagine that disease is always the outcome of, or punishment for, sin.[34] Sadly, this is *a common assumption* among chaplains and others who deal with disease. I know this from personal experience.

---

[33] Jennifer J. Freyd, *Betrayal Trauma*, 6.
[34] Larry Dossey, *Healing Words: The Power of Prayer and the Practice of Medicine*, 19.

All people who have understood their own sinfulness and accepted the forgiveness offered freely through Jesus' sacrifice naturally want others to experience the freedom and release this brings. [35] This is why Christians devote their lives to ministering in prisons, working with addicts, supporting missions, and holding Bible studies in their homes. It is the reason they gather with others to praise and worship God. They have understood and accepted the Good News, and they want to share it. This is the very foundation of our civilization, at least in principle.[36]

The *Woeful*—and this includes the average person as well as those greatly sinned against—also need this Good News. Like all people, they are sinners in need of redemption, prisoners of their own sinfulness in need of freedom and release. But they are also prisoners of the sin *of others*, bound spiritually, emotionally and often physically by the actions of others. This means they also need healing and release from the sin done to them. Tragically, they are often invisible in our congregations, their complaints seemingly unwelcome and their needs largely ignored.[37]

Healing does not come automatically when the sinned against confess their own sins; it is not a product of their being forgiven, though being forgiven can be the beginning of the journey to healing. [38] One illustration of the distinction between being forgiven and being healed is found in all three synoptic Gospels. Here it is as it appears in the book of Mark:

> Again He entered Capernaum after some days, and it was heard that He was in the house. Immediately many gathered together, so that there was no longer room to receive them, not even near the door. And He preached the word to them. Then they came to Him, bringing a paralytic who was carried by four men. And when they could not come near Him because of the crowd, they uncovered the roof where He was. So when they had broken through, they let down the bed on which the paralytic was lying. When Jesus saw their faith, He said to the paralytic, "Son, your sins are forgiven you."

[35] Harold Koenig, *The Healing Power of Faith*, 77–79.

[36] Michael McCullough, et al., *To Forgive Is Human: How to Put Your Past in the Past*, 16.

[37] Ruth C. Duck, "Hospitality to Victims: A Challenge for Christian Worship," in Andrew Sung Park and Susan L. Nelson, *The Other Side of Sin: Woundedness From the Perspective of the Sinned-Against*, 167.

[38] Robert Enright, *Forgiveness Is a Choice: A Step-by-Step Process for Resolving Anger and Restoring Hope*, 4.

And some of the scribes were sitting there and reasoning in their hearts, "Why does this Man speak blasphemies like this? Who can forgive sins but God alone?"

But immediately, when Jesus perceived in His spirit that they reasoned thus within themselves, He said to them, "Why do you reason about these things in your hearts? Which is easier, to say to the paralytic, 'Your sins are forgiven you,' or to say, 'Arise, take up your bed and walk'? But that you may know that the Son of Man has power on earth to forgive sins"—He said to the paralytic, "I say to you, arise, take up your bed, and go to your house."

Immediately he arose, took up the bed, and went out in the presence of them all, so that all were amazed and glorified God, saying, "We never saw anything like this." (Mark 2:1–12)

This encounter is rich with implications, both for forgiveness and healing. Jesus was preaching to a crowd that filled a house and spilled into the street. After four of His listeners heard His teaching, they attempted to bring their paralytic friend closer to Jesus. When they could not get themselves and the bed through the crowd, they cleverly pulled open the roof and lowered their friend next to Jesus. They had heard the Word and responded to it by faith, thinking Jesus would heal their friend. Instead, He pronounced forgiveness: "When Jesus saw their faith, He said to the paralytic, 'Son, your sins are forgiven you.'"

In doing this, Jesus challenged their understanding of who He is. The Good News of God's willingness to forgive was proclaimed, sinners in faith accepted it, and forgiveness was granted. It is a familiar pattern to modern believers, as this is exactly what sinners throughout the world have experienced, generation after generation. It is what we believe and teach about God's provision for sinners. But some present considered it blasphemy: "Some of the scribes were sitting there and reasoning in their hearts, 'Why does this man speak blasphemies like this?'" (v. 6).

Why blasphemy? Because they believed that only the sinned against, or God, can forgive sins, and since this man had not sinned against Jesus, His forgiveness of the man's sins was regarded as an assertion that He was God. And this, the scribes reasoned, was blasphemy.

The paralytic was still on his bed, not healed, and Jesus knew what the scribes were thinking, so He challenged them further: "Why do you reason about these things in your hearts? Which is easier, to say to the paralytic, 'Your sins are forgiven you,' or to say, 'Arise, take up your bed and walk'?" (vv. 8–9).

Well, which is easier to say? It doesn't take any power to simply say "your sins are forgiven you," but it clearly takes divine power to heal a paralytic and send him walking home carrying his own bed. So Jesus healed the man and proved His point: "'But that you may know that the Son of Man *has power on earth to forgive sins'*—He said to the paralytic, 'I say to you, arise, take up your bed, and go to your house'" (vv. 10–11, emphasis added).

Jesus made explicit what the scribes had reasoned in their hearts. He claimed the power to forgive sins, and He proved it by showing He had the power to do what they reasoned would be more difficult. He miraculously healed the paralytic, something they knew had to come supernaturally from God. Those present realized the implications: "All were amazed and glorified God, saying, 'We never saw anything like this.'"

Consider what had happened: The Word was proclaimed; it was accepted in faith (i.e., it was *trusted*); sins were forgiven; and next, the paralytic was healed. Scripture does not say the cause of the man's paralysis. Perhaps a birth defect, a disease, an accident, self-harm, or an injury caused by another. We do not know. But we do know that his suffering, his *Woe*, did not end with his coming to faith. His healing was a separate, subsequent and miraculous event that occurred in the presence of the power of God. It was a divine act.[39]

Scripture is replete with examples of healing at the hands of Jesus and His followers. It shows that healing is not an instant consequence of faith[40] in Jesus, though faith and healing regularly lead to each other. In the case of the blind man in John 9, his acknowledgment of Jesus as Son of God happened quite some time after his healing; in other cases, healing comes after faith; in still others, healing comes because of faith. Faith and healing are related, but not in a mechanistic, sequential, "one-size-fits-all" way.

FORGIVING ABUSERS

Back to abusers and the abused: The abused can and *must* also discover the freedom that comes from *forgiving their abusers*. This may seem counter-intuitive, but it is a key insight and means to freedom and release from Woe. Abusers must be forgiven.

But what does this mean? And why is it important? Because the wounded, and the many areas where healing is needed, are *almost always tightly bound to the perpetrator*, and victims of abuse do not receive full healing *until they choose to release themselves* from their abusers. They have

---

[39] Jeff Levin, *God, Faith and Health: Exploring the Spirituality-Healing Connection*, 183.
[40] The Greek word πίστις (*pistis*), usually translated "faith," means to *trust*, to believe in the integrity of the one speaking or acting.

33

legitimate claims against those who harmed them, and in addition to the crippling effects of the *Woe* they experience, *they are tied to their victimizers by those claims.*

A caution: This will take some time to unpack and comprehend, so tread forward deliberately and slowly. This requires considerable sensitivity, particularly if action is required to prevent further abuse of others.

Forgiveness is not usually encouraged nor forthcoming. Let's discover why.

It has long been understood by the Church and taught in Scripture that victims often desire revenge. This desire is a powerful one, and so Paul teaches:

> Repay no one evil for evil. Have regard for good things in the sight of all men. If it is possible, as much as depends on you, live peaceably with all men. Beloved, do not avenge yourselves, but rather give place to wrath; for it is written, "Vengeance is Mine, I will repay," says the Lord. Therefore "If your enemy is hungry, feed him; If he is thirsty, give him a drink; For in so doing you will heap coals of fire on his head." Do not be overcome by evil, but overcome evil with good. (Romans 12:17–21)

John Chrysostom (347–407 A.D.), in commenting on Moses' plea for Miriam's healing in Numbers 12:9–16, says:

> Miriam and her company spoke evil of Moses, and he immediately begged them off from their punishment. No, he would not so much as let it be known that his cause was avenged. But not so we. On the contrary, this is what we most desire; to have everyone know that they have not passed unpunished.[41]

That is, Moses would not even let their sin be known, but today we want the sin exposed in full public view and fully avenged. Revenge is the source of tiny family sarcasms, social-media attacks, cancel culture, blockbuster movies, gang shootings and wars. But revenge is *not* the way God directs victims to act, and it is often harmful to their own healing.

Often forgiveness is not forthcoming due to a misunderstanding of what forgiveness is. A common error is the notion that "forgiveness" is

---

[41] John Chrysostom, *Homilies on Acts 4*, reprinted in Thomas C. Owen, ed., *Ancient Christian Commentary on Scripture: Old Testament*, 3:222.

approval of the sinful act—which it is not.[42] The word used in the New Testament for *forgiveness* (ἄφεσις, *aphesis*) implies a *giving up* of a just claim, of *leaving behind* the sin or injury, of *cutting the cord* that binds the victim to the abuser.

Forgiveness is *not approving* of or *ignoring* a wrong. It is intentionally *releasing a just claim against a sinner by the sinned against*. Rightly understood, forgiveness is necessary if the sinned against are to be truly free. John Bevere calls the refusal to forgive "the bait of Satan" because it leaves its victims trapped and bound to their abuser.[43] Further, forgiving others is central not just to the healing of the abused, but also to the forgiveness of their own sins. Jesus taught this in the Lord's Prayer:

> Our Father in heaven, hallowed be your name. Your kingdom come. Your will be done, on earth as it is in heaven. Give us this day our daily bread. And forgive us our sins, as we forgive those who sin against us. (see Matt. 6:5–13)

Here, Jesus teaches us to honor the Father and move in His will, and He tells us we must forgive those who have sinned against us and toward whom we have rightful claims, if we are to be forgiven by God, who likewise has rightful claims against us. This is a constant theme in many of Jesus' parables and teachings (e.g., Matthew 5:23–24, 18:21–35), and He is unsettlingly clear that we must love those who sin against us:

> "But to you who are listening I say: Love your enemies, do good to those who hate you, bless those who curse you, pray for those who mistreat you. If someone slaps you on one cheek, turn to them the other also. If someone takes your coat, do not withhold your shirt from them. Give to everyone who asks you, and if anyone takes what belongs to you, do not demand it back. Do to others as you would have them do to you.
>
> "If you love those who love you, what credit is that to you? Even sinners love those who love them. And if you do good to those who are good to you, what credit is that to you? Even sinners do that. And if you lend to those from whom you expect repayment, what credit is that to you? Even sinners lend to sinners, expecting to be repaid in full. But love your enemies, do good to them, and lend to them without expecting to get anything back. Then your

---

[42] Robert Enright defines the meaning, scope and purpose of forgiveness in great detail and with great clarity in *Forgiveness Is a Choice*. See especially Chapter 2, "What Forgiveness Is… and What It Is Not."

[43] John Bevere, *The Bait of Satan: Your Response Determines Your Future.*

reward will be great, and you will be children of the Most High, because he is kind to the ungrateful and wicked. Be merciful, just as your Father is merciful." (Luke 6:27–36, NIV)

An Example of Forgiving and Freedom

Here's a simple example of the power of cutting the cords that bind us to another. It is small in its gravity but rightly applicable to greater burdens. Years ago I worked for a wealthy man, but I resigned to move across the country. I was still owed a paycheck for $320, and he promised to mail it to me at my new address. He never did. He knew I had no means or power to collect it, so he kept it. It was a trivial amount of money to him, but an important amount to me for rent and expenses in my new location. He had the advantage, and his greed robbed me of what was rightfully mine.

This injustice, this theft, gnawed at me for years. He grew ever more wealthy and famous, and though I succeeded and prospered in my new location and career, I never forgot nor forgave him. I was bound to him, and his sin against me had an ongoing home in my heart and mind.

That is, until I became a follower of Jesus and his teachings and example and came to understand the *power* of forgiveness. I *forgave* the man and thereby *cut the cord* that had bound me to him for all those years. I remember all the details, but the bitterness and binding are gone. I'm free from him and his sin.

This is the gift Jesus gave us in his teaching and life. Embrace it. Forgive and be free.

A Caution

All of the above is intended for the freedom, healing and sanctification for the victims of sin, including Jesus' exhortation to *love our enemies*, and to love them not just in our theology, but in our *actions*.

God says vengeance is His, not ours, so we don't seek to punish abusers to *get even*, to *get revenge*. Rather, we are commanded to *love our enemies*. Yet...

It is *not love* to allow an abuser to continue to abuse.
It is *not love* to allow a murderer to continue to kill.
It is *not love* to allow a thief to continue to steal.
It is *not love* to allow another to harm us or harm others.

It *is* love to *stop* them, *restrain* them when needed, and work *for their redemption.*

That is how we love a sinner.

5.
Making Church Safe

HEALING FOR THE SINNED AGAINST

Understanding the relationship between faith and healing is essential when ministering to the sufferers and victims of sin. All human beings suffer *Woe*. All need healing from the effects of sin committed against them.

This wounding ranges from minor to profound, but those who are wounded deeply are often the most difficult people for the Church to minister to. They are often fearful, angry, poor in relationships, self-hurting, self-medicating (generally with disastrous results), and easily triggered.[44] Often distrusting of God and anyone who has anything to do with Him, they are quick to run away, and their behavior can frustrate and exhaust people who attempt to care for them. At times it even seems they want to prove the depths of their woundedness by demonstrating how intractable it is. Ministry to plain old sinners seems easier.

A church that ministers to the sinned against must recognize the fundamentals that are central to its success, especially for the deeply wounded. These are the most important things a church must understand and incorporate in ministering to the sinned against:

- It must be safe. The full requirements of a safe environment, while beyond the scope of this book, include having windows in doors, leaving doors open, including others in counseling or prayer, asking permission to touch or hug, using appropriate language, and being authentic and ready to confess or respond to offense.[45]
- It must understand the Gospel for the *Woeful* and how they hear it.
- It must understand and teach the Gospel for sinners. The sinned against also have things in their lives they need to confess so God can forgive them.
- It must not insist or imply that the abused were complicit in the sin done to them.

---

[44] *Trigger* is a word psychologists commonly use to denote a stimulus that produces a response, often one that is unexpected in its intensity or direction. For example, someone previously mauled by a dog might react in terror in the presence of any dog. Victims of abuse often have a variety of triggers that stem from the specifics of their abuse. For example, the use of the word *Father* for God, even in a hymn, can produce profound distress during worship for someone who has been abused by a father. This does not mean we should eliminate the singing of any hymns with the word *Father* in them, but it is important to understand that triggers exist, and they can be healed.

[45] See Chapter 8, "Guidelines and Cautions."

- It must not pressure the sinned against to forgive without understanding what forgiveness is and is not.
- It must seek to have patience born not of human strength but of God. The *Woeful* (especially the deeply hurt) are seldom healed quickly, often revert to self-destructive behavior, and often quit or relapse just as everything looks greatly hopeful. This should not come as a surprise.
- It must be alert to conscious and unconscious manipulation by the *Woeful*. For them it is a method of survival, though they often apply it inappropriately.
- It must understand that God is the author and finisher of healing, not the ones who pray and certainly not their mere kindness toward those who suffer *Woe*.

Local churches, like believers, have different gifts, and some are clearly more desirous (and perhaps better equipped) to minister to the *Woeful*.[46] At other churches this is clearly not a strength, and the need is not even really perceived. They understand the Gospel as it applies to sinners, but they would find the idea of the Gospel being given for the *Woeful* strange, possibly even theologically dubious. If such churches cannot be brought into actual healing ministry—especially to the badly wounded—perhaps they can at least learn to recognize the needs of the *Woeful* and refer them to others who are better equipped to minister to them. There are churches and independent ministries who have these gifts.

HEALING AND REFUGE

When parents, clergy, teachers and others don't provide protection and healing for victims of sin, those in trouble look elsewhere for refuge and help. Often they band together for mutual support with others in similar circumstances. Many people in these groups have been abused or abandoned, often as children, and the harm done them has profoundly affected their lives as adults. Some of the abused disassociate into "parts" or personalities; some flee into the numbing refuge of alcohol or drugs. As part of the person's search for refuge from threat and pain, these choices can hardly be condemned, though they are often foolish and harmful. Those who make them are also often unaware of the Gospel or badly misinterpret it.

Many subcultures are gifted at welcoming abused individuals and making them feel safe and at home. These range from vital support groups to street gangs and can include everything from social clubs and local bars to paramilitary armies and cults. Obviously, not all such groups are harmful. As a rule, they accept the wounded far better than the Church often does, and they

---

[46] Catherine Clark Kroeger and Nancy Nason-Clark, *No Place for Abuse*, 72–74.

40

offer victims comfort, acceptance and a worldview that rightfully condemns aspects of the culture they are fleeing.

While victims of racism, disability, political oppression, poverty, slavery, abuse, sexual exploitation and myriad other kinds of suffering face similar issues, the prevalence and immediacy of the countless "alternative" communities in modern culture illustrates well the underlying challenges to the Church in healing all victims of sin.

As a whole, in its organizations and in its churches, the alternative communities are skilled at providing refuge and understanding for those who have been marginalized or abused. When others "do not want to hear about it" or don't know what to do, these communities say, "Come here. You'll be safe. We understand."

And they *do* understand. Many have suffered in a similar way, and this gives them both understanding and compassion. They empathize and readily accept abused, misunderstood and undervalued people, or anyone whose body or affect does not conform to a given cultural norm. When leaders in the Church rail against these communities without understanding why the *Woeful* see them and seek refuge there, those leaders are blind to the victims and condemn them all as sinners.

But taking refuge in some of these alternative communities can be harmful. Like other places of refuge, they can contain a "stinger"—something required for full acceptance in the community—e.g., a gang that requires "making your bones" (killing someone) for membership, a bar whose patrons must embrace alcoholism to be "one of the guys," a cult that requires rejecting one's biological family, or alternative sexual, physical, political or philosophical norms.

The tragedy is that although forgiveness and healing are the great legacy of the Church, it often seems inept and unable to deploy them. The Church should be speaking against the culture in the areas where it hurts or abandons people; instead, it often *causes* the victims' injuries or isolation. The great loss in this is that the wounded look outside the Church and *settle for refuge instead of freedom*, for empathetic acceptance of woundedness instead of healing, for (justified) anger instead of forgiveness, and for a false identity instead of their true identity in Christ.

To be fair, what victims of abuse settle for is sometimes better than what they had. This is not to say that their refuge of choice is ordained by God or without sin, but that it sees what the Church often does not: *The sins of the fathers are visited on to the third and fourth generation.*

Victims always pay for the crimes of their victimizers; victimizers pay only if caught.

As victims, the *Woeful* are fundamentally innocent, but are wounded by evil rather than complicit in it. It is not only wrong but harmful to equate their sins with the sins of those who harmed them. The sins of the latter are crimes of violence; the former, at worst, attempts to find shelter, love, and safety. Often this "misses the mark," but it is not like the sin of the abusers. It is counterproductive and *destructive* to force victims into the same category as their victimizers.[47]

For the Church to be able to minister to the *Woeful*, it must acknowledge their wounds and treat them, rather than try to force them to see themselves simply as sinners—and rather than complain that their cries of anguish disturb prayer-time. The Church must see through the wounding and see people who are made by God, living in fear, seeking refuge, and often unable to fulfill His desire for their lives. Refuge, though not God's best for us, is often better than what was, and the Church needs to see that. Jesus would see it, and He would understand. He would not leave victims of sin unhealed, hiding in refuge.

THE WOEFUL IN WAR

This analogy may help to understand the *Woeful* in relation to refuge and healing. During World War II, many people not directly involved in battle were hurt simply because the violence—shooting, bombing, stabbing—was so widespread. They often wandered the streets injured, dirty, hungry, confused and alone. Others, including the Jews, were the intentional victims of Nazi violence. All these people were true *Woeful*.

If they were fortunate in the midst of this horror, they stumbled into a partially destroyed building, where they discovered other *Woeful* hiding in a room in the basement, living as best they could with the food and supplies they found there. Sometimes Jews were hidden by non-Jewish families, who took them in, often at great personal risk. Recognizing the victims' hurt and loss, they accepted them, loved them, fed them, and shared what little they had with them.

---

[47] Those who believe in the "total depravity" of all humans (a theology of a large part of the Church) are often blind to the uncorrupted good that is in the victims of sin and to God's highest intention for each human being while here on earth. C. S. Lewis wrote, "I disbelieve that doctrine, partly on the logical ground that if we were totally depraved we should not know ourselves to be depraved, and partly because experience shows us much goodness in human nature." (*The Problem of Pain*, p. 61.) The notion of total depravity is *blasphemy*: It asserts that God's creation is evil instead of good, as He pronounced. Scripture says creation is seduced and infected by evil. The *Woeful*, as victims, are fundamentally innocent—wounded by, rather than complicit in, evil.

This was genuine, wonderful refuge, in which the battle-wounded and weary helped one another survive. They all knew they were innocent victims and the Nazis were the enemy. They knew that what the Nazis did was evil, and they hid from them. This refuge was far better than wandering the streets alone in danger and in fear—but it was still only *refuge*.

When the Allies liberated Europe and their troops entered the bombed-out towns, they found many people in hiding. Most of them willingly came out, rejoicing at their newfound freedom and ready to begin the hard task of re-envisioning and rebuilding their lives. But some, fearful of being tricked, would not come out. They believed that what they had together in refuge was better than what they would now have outside. They could not believe that something better would follow if they left their refuge and came out into the light.

Many who have been wounded in life are like that. They are *Woeful* who have found refuge in various communities (some healthy, some neutral, and some fraught with danger and further sin), and they do not want to come out. But no matter how much better their refuge is than what they suffered before they found it, Jesus would not have them remain there. The great hope of the Gospel of Jesus is for the *Woeful* to have *all* that God desires for them. He wants to heal their wounds, not just cover them over, and He wants them to find wholeness, not just have their brokenness accepted or falsely labeled "good." Ultimately, He wants the *Woeful* to leave their refuge behind and step into the light.

Jesus desires to redeem their lives and begin the process of rebuilding them into the persons God intended and desired them to be—free from wounding and free from refuge. The "stinger" in gangs, cults and other groups is that those who receive comfort there can be trapped in refuge and taught that their new identity is the end, the fulfillment of their journey to healing. This is the deception that keeps them still partially bound, and the Church must vigorously resist this deception as it seeks true healing for the sinned against.

The *Woeful* need a Liberator-Healer. To ably minister the Gospel to them, the Church must do more than use Scripture to show them they are sinners in need of a Savior or counsel them (directly or disguised as prayer) to stop sinning. Important as it is for the Church to help people realize their sinfulness, it must also minister healing to the sinned against. That requires the humility to recognize that everyone is wounded and needs healing, even though some wounding is not as profound. And never forget that those who care for the *Woeful* are also *Woeful*, in need of God's grace and healing. They are not the "holy ones" helping the unwashed. Humility is necessary.

Jesus did not rebuke and accuse the poor and suffering; He fed and healed them, and they ran to Him in response. He rebuked and accused those who considered themselves holier than the poor and suffering; those who abused, oppressed and took advantage of others; those who looked "religious" but lived selfish lives; those who expertly quoted the Law but did not live by its spirit. The way Jesus responded is how the Church, as His Body, is also to respond. This can liberate the *Woeful* by bringing them out of isolation or refuge into healing and fullness of life.

How do we do this?

6.
Foundations of How to Pray

THE SUPERNATURAL REALITY OF PRAYER

While the work of neurologists, physicians, psychiatrists, psychologists and counselors is important in healing and restoration, effective healing prayer is often absent from the recovery process. This type of prayer, which acts on its own or as a powerful catalyst to other approaches, invites the supernatural intervention of God into an individual's life and circumstances through the Holy Spirit.[48] In the same way, doctors, psychologists, therapists and other professionals can join those actively involved in the ministry of healing prayer to promote healing. All of these can be the means of God's grace, often powerfully so when all work together as a team.

Although religion and medicine have divided over the last several centuries, each often suspicious of the other, both actually have something of genuine value to offer those who need healing, and they may even be beginning to draw together again, to acknowledge each other's value and unique contribution.[49] The relation between the two began to be studied in 1902. In total, there are some 1500 studies, the vast majority of which were done within recent decades.[50]

Training is as important for those who pray for healing as it is for professionals who heal using medicine, technology or psychology.

Prayer can have little or no effect if those who pray lack understanding and training, and can in fact be dangerous, just as an untrained doctor could be. Prayer training is vital. This assertion is often met with skeptical responses like, "You mean God will ignore us if we don't get the prayer just right?"

The answer is, God listens to all prayers. But He also desires to work with and through His people in healing, and they can pray and behave in ways that render the prayer ineffective or hurtful, and thus block healing. Prayer training is, in large measure, to help those who pray learn how to "get out of the way" and allow God to work without

---

[48] Larry Dossey, *Prayer Is Good Medicine*, 49.
[49] Harold G. Koenig et al., *Handbook of Religion and Health*, 591.
[50] Ibid., 513–89.

restriction. This is quite different than the directive petitions, the perfunctory prayers, or the well-crafted but powerless words that sometimes characterize the prayers of the Church.

Healing prayer is particularly suited for the sinned against. Whatever the cause or depth of their pain, their wounding is real and must be treated as such. Nevertheless, the model of prayer for the sinned against is the same as that for those needing healing from disease, injury, addition, oppression—pretty much anything that needs healing.

THE KEY ELEMENTS OF HEALING PRAYER

The key elements of healing prayer include all or most of the following: praise, petition, invitation, listening, prophecy and blessing. To understand the process, we'll unpack each of these.

Praise is the entry into the presence of God. It is a spoken or heartfelt acknowledgment of the character and power of God. Psalm 22:3 teaches that God dwells in the praises of His people. In Romans 5:6, the word translated as "ungodly"—ἀσεβής (*asebés*)—means a *refusal* to worship or praise. Praise is not the appeasement of an angry, insecure or needy God. It is the recognition of His greatness, beauty and love. In the process of praise, those who pray begin to see and understand who God is, and this helps them pray in His will. Praise invites His presence and illuminates all prayer.

Petition is sharing one's heart and needs with God. Often, this is the only thing people pray. But in healing prayer, sometimes the real needs of those being prayed for are disguised or even unknown to them. It is not uncommon to hear a request for prayer for stress, for example, when the real need is for forgiveness, release from addiction, or healing from abuse. So while the petitioners do pray for the need that has been expressed, they also invite in the Holy Spirit.

Invitation is asking the Holy Spirit to visit right now and do whatever needs to be done. "How" the Holy Spirit manifests can take any form, including sometimes even a real, tangible presence. He can reveal what needs to be known, bring forth confession where it is needed, transport the people praying into unexpected realms, and heal what is truly wounded. The invitation to Him is without restriction: He is invited to go wherever He needs to and to uncover whatever needs to be brought to the light and healed or excised.

Listening for God's leading during the prayer will often reveal things not mentioned in the petition. Listening is paying attention to what God says to us, what He shows us, or where He leads us in further petition for the person being prayed for. A key element to (properly) listening is knowing how to discern that which is actually God speaking versus what are just our own thoughts that we might be 'projecting' onto or thinking is from God.

In 1 Samuel 3:10 (NASB), Samuel says to God, "Speak, for Your servant is listening." This is the opposite of most prayers, which are more like, "Listen, Lord, for Your servant is speaking." When those who pray invite God to lead them, speak to them, or reveal truth to them, He will do His part and honor their request. The part of the petitioners is to listen for God's instruction. This is quite distinct from presuming or imagining what God might say, and it may take time to unlearn the habit of offering advice (however well-intended) rather than listening and *keeping silent* unless clearly led to speak.

Prophecy is receiving (hearing) God's leading and acting upon it. Sometimes this is in the form of a "word of knowledge" or a "word of wisdom." Other times it is simply a deeper and more-profound love for the person being prayed for. It can also extend to a revelation of the person's life, healing, and needs, or be a forth-telling—speaking Scripture or God's love into a person's circumstances. This is sharply distinguished from letting fly "Scripture arrows," or simply quoting Scripture based on one's own motivation, agenda or theological training, or offering counseling disguised as prayer.

True prophetic leading is not from the knowledge and skill of the person praying (no matter how experienced) but from God's Spirit-revealed will.[51] This step often feels the most "supernatural," but in fact *each step* is supernatural, and they make up a profound whole.

Blessing is the final step. It is the invitation and promise for God's love and presence to fill and follow those for whom we have been praying. Just as *praise* is the opening of this time in the presence of God, the

---

[51] This is not intended to discount human experience and insight, which can clearly be gifts from God and aid in the healing process. Yet the training is such that these personal insights and experiences are explicitly surrendered and consecrated so that, if used, they might be Spirit-led. Also, at times there are things that God knows but, for His own reasons, chooses not to reveal; and there are also things He reveals to the one praying that are not intended to be shared. He also may reveal, by His choice, aspects of His foreknowledge to those who pray. For a good introduction to this, see St. Augustine, *The City of God*, 110–11. John Calvin and Duns Scotus based much of their thinking about predestination on Augustine, but they also went beyond what he discussed.

blessing is its closing and sending out, covered, filled and hopeful. It is thanksgiving for what God has done and will do.

These six steps of prayer are descriptive, not prescriptive. They are not requirements that God says must all be met or else He will not receive the prayer. No, these elements describe prayer that is humble in its access, desirous of God's leading, and focused on invitation and willingness to receive Him. Yet in a moment of crisis, the single word "Jesus." can fulfill every need in prayer.

Thus, the purpose of these guidelines is not to create a prayer legalism, but rather to help those who pray attune themselves to the work and ways of the One who heals.

THE HOLY SPIRIT AND THE CHURCH

Why is the Holy Spirit invited in healing prayer? Why not the Father or the Son? In fact, in Matthew 6:9 did not Jesus teach us to pray, "Our Father..."? Evidence of the confusion surrounding this can be found by listening to people pray. Their petitions often sound something like this: "We pray for healing, Father, for Your daughter Martha. Lord, You know how she needs You. We ask for Your filling, Holy Spirit, that she might find wholeness, yes Lord Jesus, and restoration."

Why bring this up? The purpose is not to impugn the motives of those who pray in this way, but to observe that their prayers seem to indicate a lack of understanding of *to Whom* it is we pray and *Who* acts in response.

The first issue here is the Hearer of our prayer. When Christians pray, they pray to God. They do not have to decide—as many polytheistic religions do—which of many gods is appropriate for their needs, because while Christians believe there are three Persons in the Godhead—Father, Son, and Holy Spirit—*there is only one God*. Each of these Persons is unique, and they are in eternal, self-giving, mutually glorifying relationship to one another: Three in One. The Church asserts this in the Athanasian Creed:

> We worship one God in Trinity, and Trinity in Unity; neither confounding the Persons; nor dividing the Substance. For there is one Person of the Father, another of the Son, another of the Holy Spirit. But the Godhead of the Father, and of the Son, and of the Holy Spirit is all one: the glory equal, the majesty co-eternal. Such as the Father is, such is the Son, and such is the Holy Spirit. The Father is uncreated, the Son is uncreated, the Holy Spirit is uncreated. The Father is immeasurable, the Son is immeasurable, the Holy Spirit is immeasurable. The Father is eternal, the Son eternal, the Holy Spirit eternal. And yet there are not three eternals, but one eternal. As

also there are not three uncreated, nor three immeasurable, but one uncreated, and one immeasurable. So likewise the Father is Almighty, the Son Almighty, and the Holy Spirit Almighty. And yet there are not three Almighties, but one Almighty. So the Father is God, the Son is God, and the Holy Spirit is God. And yet there are not three Gods, but one God. So the Father is Lord, the Son Lord, and the Holy Spirit Lord. And yet not three Lords, but one Lord.[52]

Thus, Christian prayer cannot be wrongly directed to one Person or another of the Trinity, because they are one almighty Lord and God. The awkward prayer above is not lost for its inelegance, nor is it more effective because it mentions all three Persons. Any Person of the Trinity is almighty Lord and God.

Why then does healing prayer focus on the Holy Spirit? Simply because Scripture teaches that He is the one given to believers for their sanctification, intercession, and filling—and because He is the one who probes the deep things of God for them:

As it is written: "Eye has not seen, nor ear heard, nor have entered into the heart of man the things which God has prepared for those who love Him." But God has revealed them to us through His Spirit. For the Spirit searches all things, yes, the deep things of God. For what man knows the things of a man except the spirit of the man which is in him? Even so no one knows the things of God except the Spirit of God. Now we have received, not the spirit of the world, but the Spirit who is from God, that we might know the things that have been freely given to us by God. These things we also speak, not in words which man's wisdom teaches but which the Holy Spirit teaches, comparing spiritual things with spiritual. (1 Corinthians 2:9–13)

The work of the Holy Spirit is further confirmed:
- In the words of Peter in 1 Peter 1:1–2: "To the pilgrims ... elect according to the foreknowledge of God the Father, in sanctification of the Spirit, for obedience and sprinkling of the blood of Jesus Christ..."
- In the words of Jesus in John 14:26: "The Helper, the Holy Spirit, whom the Father will send in My name ... will teach you all things, and bring to your remembrance all things that I said to you."

---

[52] Philip Schaff, *History of the Christian Church, Volume 3*, 689–93.

- In the words of Paul in Romans 8:26–27: "The Spirit also helps in our weaknesses. For we do not know what we should pray for as we ought, but the Spirit Himself makes intercession for us with groanings which cannot be uttered. Now He who searches the hearts knows what the mind of the Spirit is, because He makes intercession for the saints according to the will of God."

Healing prayer focuses on the Holy Spirit because Scripture teaches us that it is the role of the Holy Spirit to intercede, enlighten, fill and heal.

What If Nothing Happens?

There are times when the Holy Spirit comes in power and great healing occurs very quickly. Yet at other times, nothing seems to happen at all. At such times the Lord's presence must be sought fervently, and there must be a willingness to persist in prayer over extended periods. Those who pray must simply persist in loving those for whom they pray, knowing that the Lord determines what is required, and when, and that it may remain a mystery to us. (I know people who prayed faithfully for me for nine years before I came to faith. It is a lesson for all of us.)

Those who pray must be profoundly aware of God's love of justice. They must be humble in their requests. And they must be aware of the nagging, persistent presence of the enemy, who has held the *Woeful* captive for so long and desires to keep them bound. Satan can accomplish this by encouraging the Church to be self-righteous and cold to those who are wounded, as well as by redefining refuge as freedom. The Church must avoid both, *knowing God's delay often precedes revelation and restoration. Avoid shortcuts. Don't try to do God's work for Him.*

Experience and Training

In healing prayer, experience and solid training are essential. Surely God can do anything He pleases (and through anyone He pleases) in His healing will, but it is also incumbent upon the Church to be as well-equipped as possible to minister through healing prayer, especially in regard to understanding the dynamics and needs of the deeply sinned against.

The Church must not lump all healing into an appeal for confession, nor pressure the *Woeful* to forgive their perpetrators too quickly, though we do well to help them understand the nature of bondage that is present in resentment and unforgiveness. As Charles Finney put it:

By natural resentment I mean, that, from the laws of our being, we must resent or feel opposed to injustice or ill treatment. Not that a disposition to retaliate or revenge ourselves is consistent with the law of God. But perfect obedience to the law of God does not imply that we should have no sense of injury and injustice, when we are abused. God has this, and ought to have it, and so has every moral being. To love your neighbor as yourself, does not imply, that if he injure you, you should feel no sense of the injury or injustice, but that you should love him and do him good, nevertheless his injurious treatment.[53]

That is—just as the training teaches—resentment for injury or injustice is natural when we are abused. It is moral. God feels it as well, and it should not be brushed aside as somehow "un-Christian." But healing *will* at some point include forgiveness and the desire to love and do good to the perpetrator.

The Church needs to widen its vision of the Gospel. It is not just forgiveness for sinners—which all people need. It is also healing for the sinned against, the *Woeful*, and the Church should be as vocal and fervent in sharing this part of the Good News. It is only with both of these that the Gospel is complete.

God comforts those who have been cast down (2 Cor. 7:6), and He does this through those who love Him as they learn to love the downcast as they love themselves. As the Body of Christ, the Church must learn to love the victims of abuse and oppression (Luke 10:37). After all, in the truest sense, Jesus is the ultimate *Woeful*: Utterly innocent of any wrongdoing, He was the victim of the sin of the whole world. He is surely "a man of sorrows"[54] who fully understands all who are *Woeful*. And since we are His body in the world, we are called to love them with His love.

Loving them means offering them refuge, protecting them from further harm, standing with them against injustice, and respecting them as people made by God for love and relationship, however incompletely they now fulfill God's intentions for them. The Church's refuge, however, must not be one with a hidden stinger, a trap of further sin (or lack of complete healing) disguised as "do this because you're really one of us."

---

[53] Charles G. Finney, *Lectures on Systematic Theology,* 1851, ed. J. H. Fairchild.
[54] Isaiah 53:3.

This is a huge problem in today's culture, especially as all manner of "identity" and sexual expression are forcefully insisted upon as the "solution" to the natural body and brain development, and later hormone flows, that accompany the first two decades of life. *Everyone* experiences those changes and the discomfort they bring. Life- and body-altering interventions to impose an imagined "real you" during this season of life are both a false hope and a misdirection.

The Church must be a waystation for healing and restoration, an advocate and friend along the way toward Christlikeness, rather than a comforting environment that is actually a new deception or a trap of stagnation.

Cheap grace is no grace at all.

7.
The Practice of Healing Prayer

If you skipped the first six chapters and jumped to this chapter to get started praying for healing, don't.

From way back in Chapter 1: A friend might call and say "come on over to my house," and even if you'd never been, you might set out in the general direction and eventually find your way there. But it would be a great benefit if he gave you practical directions, told you which routes were the best, and advised "what to avoid" of muddy ravines, robbers and hornets' nests.

Scripture, history and theology will provide those directions, and will be quite practical for us. They are not unneeded extras, nor mere "theory," but valuable gifts for the traveler on this journey to God's healing presence...

Of course, there is the opposite as well—to pridefully jump into prayer not believing one needs any preparation or instruction—*refusing* to learn more about the nature and process of prayer. To proceed *that* way means that you will indeed find the hornets' nests. I have seen this happen when pride gets in the way.

So, please, if you've not already read the previous chapters, do so now. You will be guarded by following that advice.

After this, then use *Chapter 8, Guidelines and Cautions* as a summary reminder of what has been learned. You may reprint it as a handout, and it can be found on my website:

GeorgeKoch.com/HealingPrayer

Both the process below, and the guidelines and cautions listed in *Chapter 8*, have been created and enhanced over the course of many years and with the valuable learning and contribution of many prayerful individuals (many of whom are noted in the *Thanks and Acknowledgments)*. Take advantage of this experience by studying and applying what is supplied in this book.

HE ACTS, NOT US

Healing is accomplished by the invitation of our sovereign God, in the Person of the Holy Spirit, to be present and to do what only He can do.

We do not manage spiritual "forces" when we pray. We invite an encounter with the living God. He acts, not us.

STEPS IN THE PROCESS

Ask the reason for prayer: Simply: "What can we pray about?" Allow the person asking for prayer to say enough so *you* have a basic understanding of the need, but remember that the Lord *already* knows all of the details, and also that *the **real need** might not even be the one expressed.* Prayer is not a talk therapy session, so if the person goes on for more than a few sentences, gently say, "Okay. The Lord knows. Let's pray now." *And don't begin thinking of the advice you can give, or the Scripture you can recall, based on the need expressed. Your job is not to advise; it is to take this person in to be with the Lord.*

Invite: We invite the person into the presence of the Lord. Isaiah 61:1-2 reads: "The Spirit of the sovereign Lord is upon me because he has appointed me to bring good news to the poor ... to announce that captives will be released and prisoners will be freed." (We do not do the releasing and the freeing; only the Lord can do that. We announce what He is saying He will do and invite people into it.)

Submit: We invite the Lord to be in charge of the prayer session. This is what we mean when we say "Come, Holy Spirit." We lay down our own agenda for that person, our own efforts to help them, our performance needs and self-expectations, our anxiety, etc.

We turn ourselves and that person over to the Lord and ask Him to use this time to accomplish his purposes in this person's life. John 14:17 says, "He is the Holy Spirit who leads you into all truth. The world at large can't receive him because it isn't looking for him and doesn't recognize him. But you do, because he lives with you and will be in you."

Let the Holy Spirit do the leading. Look for Him and recognize Him. He is in you. He is present.

Listen: First we ask the Lord to speak and act and heal. Then we listen. *Be comfortable with silence.* Be asking the Lord to work.

Be attentive to your inner communication with the Holy Spirit, to the person being prayed for, and to the other prayer team members. (This takes practice.)

Resist the temptation to talk too much, to give God a laundry list, or *to give advice or counsel disguised as prayer, or in the form of "Scripture arrows" that you think might apply to their circumstances or sin, if there is any.* There may be a need for advice or counsel or Scripture, but *only offer it if the Lord clearly directs. He is already in them, at work. You don't need to push your way into them* with good advice, even with "religious" words, to get them on the right track. Trust Him.

Also realize that the Lord may reveal something to you, but that does not automatically mean you should say it out loud. Sometimes it is to be said right then; sometimes it is for the future; sometimes it is to give you insight and empathy but is not to be shared. *Before saying something you've been shown, ask the Lord which He intends: now, later, or never.* And if you are led to say something, offer it gently, *not being pushy or insisting that it is a word from God for them. If it is, the Holy Spirit will let them know without any pushing from you.*

SUGGESTIONS

Pray with eyes open or open them periodically:
1. This keeps you more in touch with the person being prayed for and with your team members.
2. You can watch for signs of the Holy Spirit working.

Periodically ask the person what they are experiencing.
1. Be discerning as to when to ask and when to be silent.
2. Try not to intrude on what the Lord is doing.
3. Stay connected during prayer with the person so you are not off on your own trip leaving them behind.

Don't do the Lord's job for Him.
1. *If we try to give the word of truth or comfort or conviction or guidance when the Lord wants to give it Himself, it won't have much impact.*
2. Only speak out loud things you see if you are fairly sure that the Lord is asking you to be the one to say it. In general, we would rather have the Lord say these things directly to the person through the Holy Spirit.

DEALING WITH BARRIERS

Often there will be something standing in the way of what the Lord wants to give that person. If we sense a block or barrier:
1. First (usually silently) ask the Lord to reveal it.
2. Ask the person what they are experiencing.
3. Ask if they sense a block and if they know what it is. (Often they will.)

4. Lift it up to the Lord. Ask Him what He wants to do about it. You can do this out loud.
5. Don't assume it's your job to get them past the block or figure out what it is. Don't get into performance or your expectations.
6. Listen to the Lord to see if He wants to reveal the block to you or to the person themselves. Give time. Keep interceding.
7. *If nothing seems to break, bless what the Lord is doing, bless the person and say Amen.* **He** *will follow through.*

PHYSICALITY

Touch: It is okay to hold hands, or gently "lay hands" on a person's shoulders, arms or head. At times, it is permissible to touch somewhere there is pain (with great discretion) and speak healing into it. A gentle, light touch is best.

No Massage: Do *not* massage shoulders or anything else during prayer.

Stand behind: It is not uncommon for the Holy Spirit to so fill a person being prayed for that they fall to the ground. Sometimes this is slow, sometimes fast. It is generally wise, when possible, to have one of the prayer team stand behind a person during prayer, resting hands gently on the back (just enough so they know you are there), and prepared to catch and help lower the person if they are overcome by the Spirit. If this happens, as a rule, we cover the person with a prayer cloth for modesty. There should be a stack of these where you pray.

Oil: Sometimes it is appropriate to anoint a person with oil (usually olive oil with myrrh), as a sign of blessing or anointing by God. Typically this is done with the sign of the cross, on the forehead, ears, lips, hands, or feet (seldom all of them), as led by the Spirit.

THE HOLY SPIRIT AND RELATED SCRIPTURES

When we receive salvation, our spirit is instantly and completely brought from spiritual death to eternal spiritual life. But *the flow of the Life of God* through the indwelling presence of the Holy Spirit to our human mind, will, emotions and body *can be reduced to a mere trickle by many barriers.* They fall into these general categories: our own unconfessed sin, sin that has been committed against us and the resultant wounds, resentment and unforgiveness, participation in the kingdom of darkness through the occult, various addictions and other forms of idolatry, false beliefs and misconceptions about God, and multigenerational attitudes, habits and sins. The Holy Spirit is available and eager to free us from these barriers so we can be "filled with the fullness of life and power that comes from God. Now glory be to God. By his mighty power at work within us, he is able to accomplish infinitely more than we would ever dare to ask or hope" (Eph. 3:19b, 20). Following are some verses that illustrate how Scripture applies to different aspects of healing.

Our human spirit is made alive in Christ

+ *Romans 8:10*, "Since Christ lives within you, even though your body will die because of sin, your spirit is alive because you have been made right with God."

Our human soul (mind, will, emotion) can be touched by the Holy Spirit

+ *2 Corinthians 4:16*, "Therefore we do not lose heart. Though outwardly we are wasting away, yet inwardly we are being renewed day by day."
+ *Ephesians 3:16*, "I pray that from his glorious, unlimited resources he will give you mighty inner strength through his Holy Spirit. And I pray that Christ will be more and more at home in your hearts as you trust in him. May your roots go down deep into the soil of God's marvelous love. And may you have the power to understand, as all God's people should, how wide, how long, how high, and how deep his love really is. May you experience the love of Christ, though it is so great you will never fully understand it."

The effect of the Holy Spirit on our human mind

+ *Romans 12:2*, "Don't copy the behavior and customs of this world, but let God transform you into a new person by changing the way you think. Then you will know what God wants you to do, and you will know how good and pleasing and perfect his will really is."
+ *Romans 8:6*, "If your sinful nature controls your mind, there is death. But if the Holy Spirit controls your mind, there is life and peace."

The effect of the Holy Spirit on our human will

+ *Romans 8:9*, "But you are not controlled by your sinful nature. You are controlled by the Spirit if you have the Spirit of God living in you."
+ *Revelation 3:20*, "Look. Here I stand at the door and knock. If you hear me calling and open the door, I will come in, and we will share a meal as friends."
+ *Romans 8:12-13*, "So, dear Christian friends, you have no obligation whatsoever to do what your sinful nature urges you to do. For if you keep on following it, you will perish. But if through the power of the Holy Spirit you turn from it and its evil deeds, you will live."

The effect of the Holy Spirit on our human emotions

+ *Isaiah 61:1-3*, "The Spirit of the Sovereign Lord is upon me, because the Lord has appointed me to bring good news to the poor. He has sent me to comfort the brokenhearted and to announce that captives will be released and prisoners will be freed."

+ *Psalm 34:4*, "I prayed to the Lord, and he answered me, freeing me from all my fears."

+ *1 Peter 5:7*, "Give all your worries and cares to God, for he cares about what happens to you."

+ *Isaiah 49:13b*, "For the Lord has comforted his people and will have compassion on them in their sorrow."

The effect of the Holy Spirit on our human body

+ *Romans 8:11*, "The Spirit of God, who raised Jesus from the dead, lives in you. And just as he raised Christ from the dead, he will give life to your mortal body by this same Spirit living within you."

+ *Luke 6:19*, "Everyone was trying to touch him, because healing power went out from him and they were all cured."

QUICK LIST OF DO'S AND DON'TS IN HEALING PRAYER

DO:
- Ask the person to say briefly why prayer is sought.
- Ask permission to touch. See *Chapter 8.*
- Pray with this basic PRAYER MODEL in mind:
  - Invite the Holy Spirit's presence
  - Ask what the need is, if known
  - Praise God (in spoken words or song)
  - Petition: speak out the need
  - Listen: speak only if you get leading
  - Bless
- Allow silence.
- Try to keep a balance of gender (if you see a prayer person alone praying with a member of the opposite gender, find a way to balance it).
- Speak words if you get them, but gently.
- Intercede inwardly if someone else is praying aloud.

DON'T:
- Get into a long conversation about what to pray for.
- Give advice or do counseling, or use "Scripture arrows."
- Talk too much.
- Rush to fill in silences.
- Pray one-on-one with the opposite gender.
- Pray if you have an active addiction.
- Force "words" on people by tone of voice or demeanor. If it really is from God, the Holy Spirit will do the convicting. It's not our job.

8.
Guidelines and Cautions

As new people come into our congregations, small groups, fellowships and meetings, we need to occasionally review some of the standards of touch, respect, leadership, language and caution that will help make our gathering a very safe place. This is extraordinarily important, because we are called to be a sanctuary and healing oasis for the ill and injured, and especially for those who have been victims of abuse.

Normal, friendly hugging and touching are central to the love and affection that characterizes a healthy gathering. Nothing in these guidelines and cautions is meant to dampen these expressions of affection. It would be foolish, however, not to recognize that there are some ways of touching, speaking, meeting and leading that are appropriate, and others that are not.

Some individuals appreciate and seek most any kind of appropriate touch, but for others this is uncomfortable, painful or frightening. It is very important, especially with new people, that we do not become overly familiar—hugging or touching—unless clearly invited. A warm greeting and a bright, genuine smile will touch people's hearts, and are more appropriate, when someone is new, than a "familiar" hug or touch. Some folks, even long-term members or friends, do not welcome being hugged. This boundary is legitimate and should be respected. We should not push them to "get over it" and hug or touch us because we think it'll be good for them. *We need to show respect.*

Any *inappropriate* touch can have unholy consequences: It can leave a person feeling hurt, violated, disrespected, and fearful of even being present with us. Even when unintended, the consequences can be profound, especially with people who have suffered physical, emotional or sexual abuse.

It is our responsibility—*all* of us—to be gentle and aware of our actions. And we must all be willingly accountable to each other, as we are to God.

So, if you see someone engaged in what might be perceived as inappropriate touch (or humor, language, look, "grooming," forced closeness or intimacy—or any other such behavior, for that matter), whether it appears intentional or not, *immediately* take them aside and share your concerns in a *caring* but clear manner. This is a mutual accountability that we should each welcome. Also inform someone in leadership right away.

The goal here is not to produce a politically correct police-state, with everyone informing on everyone, and feeling "watched" for the least little supposed impropriety. The goal here is to preserve the integrity and love, and not let it be damaged or destroyed by anyone—in a position of leadership or not—whose actions are inappropriate and hurtful. Inappropriate touch, language or action should be quite rare, but they should *never* go unnoticed or unattended to. Our gatherings should be the safest place on earth.

In this light, here are some guidelines and cautions. These are not intended to be exhaustive, but illustrative, to provide direction:

- Avoid sexual humor or innuendo.
- Avoid touching others between the waist and the knees with any part of your body. Do not touch females on the chest.
- Do not kiss people on the lips. This is common in some cultures, but not in others, except within an immediate family or with some long-term, close friends (and in some subcultures). A kiss on the cheek is acceptable for people who invite it. Ask permission if you are unsure.
- Do not stroke or caress in any way that might be perceived as erotic or overly familiar. (Giving someone a neck or shoulder rub, if they desire it and it is done appropriately, is usually acceptable.) BUT...
- Do not massage at all while you are laying hands on someone for prayer. It is confusing and distracting.
- Do not press your whole body close to someone during a hug, nor sustain a hug for more than a few seconds, nor squeeze so firmly that a person might feel trapped or constrained.
- Youth leaders are not to invite any teen or child to any outside event without parents' explicit permission. If an emergency requires you give a ride home to a young person, ensure the parents know in advance and approve, and that other adults know the ride is about to take place. Do not make any detours; go straight to the child's home. Make sure they are safely inside before leaving.

Background checks must be conducted for everyone in any official leadership role or working with children and teens. Again, we want our gathering to be the safest place on earth.

Any attempt to engage a minor in any sexual relationship must be reported immediately to the police.

Both youth and adult leaders should be genuine and natural, but always aware that their actions and words set an example that either brings glory or discredit to God. As believers, we respect and love each other regardless of age, race, gender, income or national origin.

Immature, unchristian or inappropriate actions or words may result in removal from leadership. Our love for God and our care for each other should be our primary hallmarks.

God is love. We are clearly called to express God's love toward each other. Our society is so confused about love and eroticism that we must not allow anything to deepen that confusion.

Neither should we allow anything to inhibit genuine and appropriate touch, affection, prayer or counsel, especially with the deep care that members demonstrate for each other. If you are ever uncertain, ask this: *How would Jesus touch? How would Jesus counsel? How would Jesus lead? What would Jesus do?* Use Jesus as your guide. And willingly and readily seek counsel if you are not sure, or need clarity.

A profound and genuine kindness should characterize our interactions with anyone who suffers. It simplifies our prayer and our love, and softens the heart that is hurting.

SUPPLEMENTARY MATERIALS

Appendix A:
Stories of Real Healings

What follows is a series of anecdotal tellings of real healings. Anecdote is not proof, and not usually able to be subjected to scientific inquiry where alternative explanations can be tested and verified. But this doesn't make it untrue. It is history, told with as much accuracy and honesty as possible, and we can learn from it.

Every telling here is either from my own personal experience with healing prayer, or from someone I know personally and trust. Each is written in the first person, but the one telling the story is not identified, and names have been changed to protect those who were present. With that said, these are true stories. With time and prayer you will have (and may already have) many of your own. Share them. Testimony encourages faith.

1. AFTER GRACIE

The lead supervisor in my chaplaincy training had begun the year with an introductory talk that included this directive: "You have twenty seconds after you enter a patient's room to discern what sin is at the root of their disease or injury." I was taken aback, and I remembered what Jesus had said:

> Now as Jesus passed by, He saw a man who was blind from birth. And His disciples asked Him, saying, "Rabbi, who sinned, this man or his parents, that he was born blind?" Jesus answered, "Neither this man nor his parents sinned, but that the works of God should be revealed in him." (John 9:1–3)

So I spoke up: "I have a three-year-old son who has epilepsy. Who sinned?"

The supervisor looked at me, rolled his eyes and said, dismissively, "You just don't get it."

Needless to say, I was not the favorite student from that day forward. But though I didn't know it, this changed after Gracie's healing (see Chapter 1) and the experience of the presence of the Holy Spirit by all of us, when she and I prayed.

Toward the end of the course, the supervisor said he needed to talk to all of us, that his time of leading this course was likely coming to an end.

He'd had a heart attack over the weekend while gardening. He had been examined in the emergency room, had many tests and scans, and was told that surgery was necessary to repair the damage that had been done. It was to be Thursday of that week.

We were all sitting in our big circle in the room, stunned, when he then looked directly my way and said, "George, will you pray for me?"

I jumped out of my chair and ran across the room to him, laid hands and began to pray. The chairs all emptied. Everyone gathered close and laid hands on him, or on others who had hands on him. It was a massive response. We prayed for healing.

After a few minutes he thanked us, and we all headed our separate ways. The following week when we returned to the meeting room, he was there. Once we had all settled in, he reminded us of the previous week and his surgery. He said the surgeons had begun their procedure, but suddenly stopped, withdrew, and said, "The damage is gone. You do not need surgery. Your heart is fine." They sent him home, and he came to share with us this final miracle.

What a year that was for all of us.

2. "I HATE YOU"

I was working as a chaplain at a county hospital in a major city. These hospitals are the landing pads for the marginalized and criminals when they get sick, and they are tough duty for all who work there.

Earlier in the morning I'd been asked to bring a Bible up to the high-security psych ward. People dangerous to themselves and others were housed there and guarded, including those deemed "criminally insane." The guard at the entrance took the Bible and told me that the patient who had requested it was now asleep, but he would see that it got delivered.

Hours later, I was called again. The same patient wanted to meet with me. I went up to the floor, through the "mantrap." (A door opens into a tiny room, then locks behind you. You are carefully observed and quizzed. The next door leads from the tiny room to the ward.) I walked onto the floor, and an attendant went to get the patient, who was eating lunch with the other patients.

He got up and began to walk toward me. He was tall, wearing a prison jumpsuit, carrying his food tray. As he approached me, I could see he still had food around his mouth, and he walked stiffly, like an awkward robot.

He came and stood right in front of me, close, stiff, towering, staring down, and through clenched teeth and a quivering jaw, in a deep and menacing voice, he said very slowly, "I ... HATE ... YOU." It felt genuinely as if he was being animated and directed by a demon living inside of him.

I was in real danger. It would take but a second or two for him to injure or even kill me. But I felt oddly calm—not a false bravado, but rather like I was surrounded by a column of the Holy Spirit—and completely protected.

I asked, "Do you want to talk?"

He nodded stiffly, and we walked over to a couch and chair. I sat in the chair, and he sat stiffly on the couch. He put the tray down, and I asked him about himself. Seeming to fight to get words out through an uncooperative body and mouth, he told me of his rough childhood, his troubles with the law since youth, his incarcerations, and his hopelessness.

I might have been tempted to address the demon that really seemed to co-reside in him and which fought his efforts to talk to me, but instead I found myself asking him if he had ever known about or accepted the love of Jesus. He said no. He wasn't even sure what that meant.

I briefly shared the Gospel: God loved him, Jesus had given Himself for him, and there was freedom from all of his past, his abuse, his crimes, his sin. Would he like to try? He said yes.

I led him through a simple prayer. I spoke and he repeated, sentence by sentence, something like this: "God, I'm sorry for all I've done that was wrong. Please forgive me. Jesus, I want You in my life to lead me. Please come into my heart." What happened next surprised both of us.

There *was* a demon, and it left like a rocket shooting out of his body. Jesus *had come in*. It *had to leave*.

There was a deep sigh, and his body turned to rubber and sank into the couch. There was great relief and astonishment on his face. He just sat there for a minute, stunned by this new reality.

Finally he turned to me and asked, "Was it always this easy?"

I smiled and answered, "Yes."

He laughed and said, "Wow."

After another minute he said, "Now what do I do with the rest of my life?" We talked about finding a local community of believers, finding a way to serve, and simply going forward step-by-step in his new life in Christ.

3. ON THE WAY DOWN THE MOUNTAIN

I have a badly injured knee, from the splintering of my tibia playing baseball many years ago. The meniscus is shredded, and I get viscous injections in it once or twice a year. It often hurts when the weather changes or if I overuse it or bang it against something. Still, I like to hike, will sometimes put a brace on it, and I persist in living life with the injury. Surgery someday? Maybe. Healing? I'd love it. But it continues to be a pain and a minor threat.

We lived near the base of a small mountain, and one afternoon I decided on a solo hike up into the trees for some fresh air and good exertion. As the day grew late and evening was approaching, I realized I needed to head back down toward home. Everything seemed fine as I descended and then suddenly, I stepped between boulders and wrenched the knee badly. It hurt like heck, and I could no longer walk on it. The support was gone, and the pain was high.

I sat down at the base of a tree. The weather wasn't bad, and I figured I was in for a wait. There were no cell phones in those days, but eventually my family would become concerned, would notify authorities, and they would come looking for me—though maybe not until the next morning. Dusk was settling in. I hurt a lot and couldn't walk any farther, but I could wait.

It came to me then that I was a person who willingly prayed for the healing of other people, and I'd seen God heal many times. I had a crazy idea: I could pray for myself as I had for others. I wondered, of course, *Can ya **do** that? Isn't that a little too selfish and weird?* But I did it anyway.

I put both hands on my knee and asked God to heal it. *Instantly* the pain was gone. I think I jumped a little bit at the shock. I stood up and tentatively tried the knee. It held. The prayer worked. It was the opposite of the placebo effect because I expected nothing to change. But it did. I was back to normal, and I wandered the rest of the way down the mountain.

4. THE GIRL WITH THE CURVED SPINE

I'd never prayed for anyone's healing. I think I believed God could heal if He chose, but I hadn't seen it in person. The phone rang, and some dear friends asked me to come over and help them pray for their daughter. I think she was perhaps eight or nine at the time. She had scoliosis, and she was lying on her bed face-down when I came into the room. Her lower spine was in an odd S-shape, and she was crying from the pain of it.

None of us had experience in healing prayer, but we stood on both sides of her and gently touched her back. We prayed and prayed that God would straighten her spine, relieve her pain, and heal her.
Before our very eyes we saw something we never expected and that astonishes me to this day: Her spine straightened *out as we watched.* The pain vanished. She was healed.

In that moment I believed in God's willingness and supernatural ability to heal. I believed it. I believe it now.

5. THE FOUR-YEAR-OLD GIRL LEFT TO DIE

I was a chaplain in a major city hospital. During rounds one day I stopped by the Pediatric ICU and was chatting with the nurses at the station. I noticed one of the rooms had the lights off and a small child's bed sitting in the middle of it. I asked what that was about, and the nurses told me it was a sad day. A four-year-old girl had no hope of recovery, had been taken off life support, and placed in the quiet dark room to pass away. They expected her death within a few hours. I don't know where her family was.

I asked, "Would it be all right if I went in and prayed for her?"

The nurses there were kind, understanding, dedicated and all of them, as far as I could tell, believed in God and appreciated chaplains. I've had that same experience and impression with all the nurses (and doctors) I've encountered over the years. They said, "By all means. Go. Pray." And so I did.

The young girl was sleeping peacefully and unmoving. I held a hand in the air over her and simply asked God to heal her. It was a simple prayer and not long. I was grateful to be with her, but I also accepted what the nurses had told me. She was dying.

The next day, I returned to the same ward, went up to the nurses' station, and saw that the same room was now empty and the lights were on to full brightness. I assumed the girl had passed on. But I asked, "What happened to the little girl that was in that room yesterday?"

"Oh, *her.* She didn't die. She woke up and is completely fine. She went home with her family."

I was stunned, speechless.

My, how God is good.

6. ADOPTED THEN GONE

The boy was young. Under 3. His older parents had adopted him after never being able to have a child of their own. They loved him and relished his little life growing to be a part of theirs.

One evening, in the living room, eating grapes with them, the boy choked. A grape had lodged in his windpipe. He couldn't breathe. His parents called 911 but couldn't dislodge the grape. By the time the paramedics arrived, he was unresponsive. After a Heimlich maneuver he was breathing again but still unconscious.

I met them in the Pediatric ICU. They were frightened and he was very still. We talked. I prayed. I asked for healing and recovery and long life. No response.

The boy remained in the hospital for another few weeks. I came regularly to pray for him: with the parents if they were there, just for the boy if they weren't. I prayed every way I knew how. No response.

Eventually he was moved to another hospital, a little over an hour away. I drove there as well. Prayed again. Exhorted God to intervene and raise this boy up. No response.

Soon after, he was gone. The breathing stopped, and he died. His parents were grief-stricken and inconsolable. I comforted and prayed, but their small son was gone.

This all happened decades ago, and it still is very present to me. I have seen miraculous healings many times. And yet there are times when God does not act as I hope and desire.

I wish I had a good explanation, but I don't. I know He is God, and He chooses. And those choices will sometimes confuse and sadden us. For now I leave it there, trusting Him even when I do not understand.

7. GO TO JESUS

Usually when I pray for someone in the hospital it's for healing, often for comfort, often for comfort for the family. Yet one time a nurse approached me on the ICU floor and pointed to a family gathered around a man in one of the bays. He was probably in his forties and was unconscious.

The nurse said, "He's septic. Everything is bad. Organs failing, yet the mother will not stop begging him not to die, and he is hanging on."

The rest of the family was standing outside, confused, at their wit's end, having no idea what to do.

I went into the room, and the mother was talking to her son about the wonderful food she was going to make him when he came home from the hospital.

I might have otherwise then approached and prayed for his healing, but I knew this was not what was ahead. He was ready to die but was being "held back" by his mother. I *know* that sounds strange, but that's what was going on.

I spoke to her quietly and told her to go and be with her family, that she had to let him go to Jesus, and I would be out in a few minutes. She understood and left the room.

I walked up close to him and spoke quietly in his ear, "It's okay. You can go. The family will be all right. Go to Jesus." Almost immediately his body relaxed, and his breathing stopped. He was with Jesus.

I went out and talked to the family, explained what had just happened, and invited them all back into the room, where I conducted a time of prayer with them. I told them each to go up to him and say goodbye, and they each kissed him on the forehead and said goodbye.

There were many tears, but the comforting presence of God was with them all. It was a true healing.

Appendix B:
Healing's Forgotten History

For those who desire an understanding of the history and practice of healing, this appendix reviews relevant writings on the subject, particularly within the Judeo-Christian context, and how we apply them in teaching healing prayer.

The word *healing* is used in many ways in literature, research, apologetics, medicine, psychology, everyday speech. The focus here is "divine healing"—healing that occurs without apparent physical cause and stems from God's supernatural intervention in a person's life to partially or completely replace disease or disorder with well-being. [1] A basic assumption in this review, as in my doctoral study, is that both the Old and New Testaments, and the history of the Christian Church to this day, testify that God heals.

Abundant contemporary literature is available on the topic of healing, and it is represented in this chapter. However, little of it is focused on training people to pray with others for healing (the focus of this book), and little of it seems cognizant of the testimony of the Church or early history (one of the concerns of this appendix). Since the purpose here is to examine literature that focuses on how and when God heals and what conditions might aid or hinder the progress of this healing, the scope of related literature will be intentionally broad—encompassing some 8000 years— and will incorporate considerable reference to Scripture, as well as the literature of the Christian church from the first century to the present. This review will consider several aspects of the literature, including the kinds of healing God effects, the evidence of its occurrence throughout history, and the understanding of God and healing that it reflects.

HEALING FOCUS IN CONTEMPORARY LITERATURE

Healing is a response from God commonly mediated by a human being. It is a response to disease or damage of some sort, either by accident or abuse. By accident is meant without human intention (whether a falling tree or a virus), and by abuse is meant the intentional acts of humans against others or themselves. While the victims of accidents also need

---

[1] Many people, ranging from strict materialists who deny the existence of anything supernatural to cessationists, reject even the possibility of divine healing. An examination of such objections is not without merit, but it is beyond the scope and purpose of this review.

healing, much of the contemporary literature on healing deals with the victims of different kinds of abuse.[2]

Abuse is sin, and sin always has a victim. Sin is an abuse of what God has made, and it causes wounding that persists until it is healed. Today it seems as if abuse is pandemic. All around us we see evidence of racial, sexual, social, familial, physical, emotional, religious and other kinds of abuse. Whether it has always been widespread is a topic of much speculation and little knowledge. Perhaps what was common but hidden has now simply been exposed. It may be that *abuse* is simply a new word applied to an old reality—sinner and sinned against.

Regardless, abuse is a reality for a large number of people, and many of them have been emotionally and otherwise crippled by it. Understanding the nature and range of abuse is vital to understanding the depth and need of healing for its victims. Perhaps that is why the contemporary literature focuses on the most salient examples of abuse in society today.

One obvious area of abuse is racism. Racism, which has occurred worldwide throughout history, stems from a fundamental fear of the other, as I have observed elsewhere:

> A defining characteristic of human society is its tribalism: its tendency to gather in groups which define themselves by certain common characteristics, and differentiate themselves—set themselves apart from and at odds—with other groups and individuals who do not share these characteristics.[3]

This fear of the other is seen widely in the animal, plant and insect kingdoms, and while it may have served a purpose in preserving life in some species, today it manifests itself primarily in unnecessary, destructive acts by humans toward other humans.[4]

Racism is one of those acts. It is almost self-evidently irrational, or perhaps nonrational, meaning that it stems from a part of our brains that are below rational thought. In *Black Like Me*, a white man who had dyed himself dark brown exposed how this blinding prejudice seemed to work:

> I learned within a very few hours that no one was judging me by my qualities as a human individual and everyone was judging me by my pigment. As soon as white men or women saw [us]...they saw us as

---

[2] Some people consider accidents just part of life's natural struggle. Others regard God as their author or as letting them occur. Regardless of the theory of their ultimate origin, the effects of "accident" can be destructive to body and soul and will often lead the victims to seek healing. However, those who blame God often avoid seeking Him for healing, regarding Him as the problem, not the solution. Likewise, those who regard accidents as merely natural events often avoid seeking healing from God because they either disbelieve in Him or think Him unwilling or unable to heal them.

[3] George Koch, "Investigative Paper on Fear of the Other." www.georgekoch.com/articles/Fear_of_the_Other.htm

[4] Gerald L. Sittser, *Loving Across Our Differences*.

"different" from themselves in fundamental ways: we were irresponsible; we were different in our sexual morals; we were intellectually limited. ... We had the feeling that the white person was not talking with us but with his image of us.[5]

The "image" others have of us goes to the heart of much of healing ministry, both because it skews our relationship with others and because we often adopt it as our own self-image. People who have been told they are inferior, or who have been treated in abusive ways, often accept these attitudes as the truth about themselves. This is exacerbated when purveyors of racist ideas claim biblical and scientific authority for their notions. In *Race, Religion and Racism*, Frederick Price exposes and eviscerates such claims, such as these from Charles Carroll:

We are able with the assistance of Scriptures and the sciences to determine that the Negro is one of the ape family; that he simply stands at the head of the ape family...he is merely an ape. ... Besides, it should be borne in mind that, though the Negro is omnivorous, he manifests a strong preference for the flesh of man as an article of food. The ... Negro [is] the creature described in the Scripture as the "beast of the field."[6]

The horror of such illogic is profound, but the attitude it reflects is still with us, widely embraced in spirit, if not in degree. Although in the United States racism is universally thought of first in terms of white versus black, it takes many other forms: white ("us") versus Hispanic, Asian, Jewish, Italian, Irish, Eastern European, and all suspect categories ("them"). The Korean-American community often sees itself as the target of racism from both the white and black communities. During the Los Angeles riots in 1992, for example, black rioters set fire to 2500 stores in Koreatown. Repeated calls to the Los Angeles Police Department brought no response.[7] Racism knows no color or cultural boundaries, and it remains a pervasive problem in American society, *and in virtually every other culture in the world and in history.*

Ronald C. Potter expresses this conviction this way:

New macroeconomic realities coupled with an unprecedented ethical and spiritual crisis with African-American communities have rendered implausible the thesis that white racism is the sole impediment to black social progress.

---

[5] John Howard Griffin, *Black Like Me*, 180.
[6] Charles Carroll, *The Tempter of Eve*, 286–87, in Frederick K. C. Price, *Race, Religion and Racism,* vol. 2, 5–6.
[7] Andrew Sung Park, *Racial Conflict and Healing*, 21–22.

Notwithstanding its changing contours, however, the American dilemma remains this nation's foremost ethical, political and ecclesial problem.[8]

Fear of the other is pervasive, but it is also particular. Words and actions focus fear on a certain kind of person, and the fear is reinforced in both the racist and the target of racism. In reporting on their co-pastorate at a racially integrating church, two pastors, one black and one white, observed that victims of racism were "shy" and retreated from human contact, behavior that is also typical of victims of abuse.[9]

Healing is needed both for the victims of racism and the perpetrators of it. But just as a person will not heal fully from a history of sexual abuse until it is acknowledged, so too will the Church not heal of its racism—nor will the victims heal of its effects—until it is admitted frankly.[10] The perpetrators must see the lie and confess the abuse. For the victims of racism, there must be healing from both the wounding suffered and the broken image of who they are. God's healing is needed to enable them to reject the racist's opinion of their worth and to *reveal the masterpiece they are in His eyes:* "For we are God's masterpiece. *He has created us anew in Christ Jesus, so that we can do the good things he planned for us long ago*" (Ephesians 2:10, NLT).

The approval or passive allowance of the source of pain must also be addressed, both personally and in its social expression. Simply making victims of racism feel better about themselves—and even fully healed— does not eliminate the root cause of racism in society. Society's acquiescence in racism must also be exposed and repudiated.

In *Betrayal Trauma*, Jennifer Freyd makes this same case in reference to victims of sexual abuse.[11] Sexual abuse is a common topic in contemporary literature. The sexual abuse of boys by Roman Catholic priests has recently figured prominently in the press. As detestable as these acts are, they demonstrate the truth of the scriptural witness of sin being passed from generation to generation (see Chapter 2). The abusers were often abused themselves, and the child-abusing sexuality of the priests is a common outcome of that abuse. The current social climate has led many people to reject even cogent discussions of the issue. Further, long-term scientific studies are hard to come by, and some are only recently bearing fruit.[12]

---

[8] Ronald C. Potter, "Race, Theological Discourse and the Continuing American Dilemma," chapter 2 of Dennis Okhom, *The Gospel in Black and White*.
[9] Spencer Perkins and Chris Rice, *More Than Equals*, 24.
[10] Ibid., 91.
[11] Jennifer J. Freyd, *Betrayal Trauma*, 170–71.
[12] R. Timothy Kearney, *Caring for Sexually Abused Children*, 123.

Nevertheless, people who have ministered to victims of sexual abuse understand these realities.

Victims of sexual abuse are often bound by a false or broken image of who they are.[13] Healing ministry is thus aimed to restore the image of God in which these people were made, and to *replace the broken and false image that others have forced upon them and which they have often accepted.* Of course, this is not just a matter of "changing your mind." *These broken images are so real and so ingrained that it requires the supernatural power of God to heal them.*

Perhaps worse than broken images in victims of abuse is the deliberate forgetting they do to survive. Victims forget—on purpose—even when the wounding is still unhealed. And *while this allows the victims to "get on with life," it also warps their views of others and of themselves, creating self-destructive patterns whose roots are hidden, but whose fruits are bitter and often obvious.*[14] A distorted sexuality is commonly one of the fruits directly tied to the betrayal by a parent or other adult who uses the child for gratification (or the object of anger). It is not the only root. But it is a common one. It is well known and understood by those who deal with victims of abuse.

Other fruits of sexual abuse include promiscuity, lack of appropriate personal boundaries, self-mutilation, introversion, icy relationships, depression, agoraphobia, hatred, anger and rejection.[15] The list is almost endless.

Physical abuse takes many forms. Except in extreme cases, the body heals from it in time, but often the soul does not. The wounding that manifests itself outwardly as a bruise, a cut, a broken bone, or a violation (as in rape) will often heal without significant long-term physical effect. But when the attack is intentional and the abuser is known, *there is also a deep wounding of the inner person, and this often initiates a spiral of fear, brokenness, self-condemnation and retreat.*

Joyce Meyer tells the story of a 4-year-old boy who earnestly desired to play soccer. He practiced relentlessly and then went out to play his first game. Halfway through the game—in which he seemed to be doing fine—a "big kid" came up to him and punched him hard in the stomach. "You're not doing anything right." he yelled. "You get off this field and don't come back here and try to play with us anymore."[16] Later, after he had returned home and the physical pain had passed, the boy declared that he would never go back. The

---

13 Leanne Payne, *The Broken Image.*
14 Freyd, especially chapter 4, "Why Forget?"
15 Mario Bergner, *Setting Love in Order.*
16 Joyce Meyer, *The Root of Rejection,* 15–16.

wound to his soul persisted, and it might well have killed his desire to ever play any sport again. "This is a perfect example of what the devil wants to do to people," Meyer concludes. "He wants to get somebody to reject us."

No Place for Abuse, by Catherine Clark Kroeger and Nancy Nason-Clark, looks at the tawdry record of the Church in response to widespread violence against women and young girls. The authors quote the Surgeon General that the single greatest cause of injury for women in the United States is domestic violence, whose victims exceed the combined total victims of traffic accidents, rapes, and muggings.[17] These statistics are open to criticism, as this entire issue has been highly politicized.[18] But whatever the true number of victims, there is a real problem. One man (apparently a deacon in the Church) said:

> You cannot stand the order of creation on its head. Only the man is the Lord of Creation, and he cannot allow himself to be dominated by womenfolk. So hitting has been my way of marking—that I'm a man, a masculine man, no softie of a man, no cushy type.[19]

Many church leaders would cringe at such an outlandish and repulsive assertion, but it is a fact that many men beat their "womenfolk," as attested to by the Surgeon General's report and as witnessed by many in the work of healing ministry.

While much of the public debate focuses on physical violence against women and girls, violence against men and boys is also real. They are abused by mothers, wives, sisters, fathers, neighbors, coaches, gym teachers, peers, sexual partners, and others. It could well be underreported, as those in healing ministry often discover, only after significant trust has been built, that physical abuse has been part of a man's history.

Lastly, crime is a source of significant physical abuse that injects terror into a person's waking and sleeping hours even long after the crime. Dan Allender recounts the story of a pastor friend whose brother was murdered, shot in the head by a stranger, and how this stifled the pastor's ability to do anything with God other than yell at Him.[20] In another instance, thieves robbed a woman's house and destroyed things apparently just for their own pleasure. She

---

[17] Catherine Clark Kroeger and Nancy Nason-Clark, *No Place for Abuse*, 67.
[18] "Spousal Abuse of Men," AFU and Urban Legend Archive, http://www.urbanlegends.com/misc/spousal_abuse_of_men.html
[19] Kroeger and Nason-Clark, *No Place for Abuse*, 119, quoting Eva Lundgren, "'I Am Endowed with All the Power in Heaven and on Earth': When Men Become Men Through 'Christian' Abuse," *Studia Theologica: Scandinavian Journal of Theology* 48.1.
[20] Lisa Barnes Lampman and Michelle D. Shattuck, *God and the Victim*, chapter 3.

recounted how it made the house feel unclean and unsafe. Allender comments, "If evil can destroy faith, hope, and love, then, in fact, it has to a large degree debilitated our capacity to function in the world, in relationships, and on behalf of God and others."[21]

To be sure, false memory, mental disease or attempts at manipulation can lead to false claims of abuse, but that should not lead the Church to sequester itself in denial or cling to a theology that focuses on the sinner and renders the sinned against nearly invisible.[22] Real people are really hurt, and it breaks not just their skin or bones, but their souls. The wounds to the soul persist long after the body heals, and they must cease to be invisible in our churches for healing to occur.

Abuse seldom falls into one neat category. When people are willing to abuse— to disrespect and harm others—they commonly use a variety of means. When any abuse takes place, emotional abuse is always present. It is the wounding of the soul as a consequence of the act of abuse. However, it can also stand alone. Some abusers harm their victims merely by using words to demean and belittle them. They do this to make their victims comply with their wishes and because the act of abuse and the suffering of the victim give them feelings of pleasure and superiority. This sort of control is typical in cults.[23] It is also found in highly authoritarian families and in some cultures.

Emotional abuse can be damaging even when it is passive. In *Healing the Wounded Spirit,* John and Paula Sandford tell of an anorexic young woman who suffered from depression, overwhelming guilt, and extreme perfectionism. The abuse she suffered was passive: There was no affection between her parents or toward her. They told her she had been an accident, and even though her father tried to have "intellectual" conversations with her, he belittled her efforts.[24] Their failure to connect with and affirm this woman when she was a child was passive, but the effect of the abuse was debilitating into her adulthood. This is emblematic of the power of any kind of abuse to cripple a person's capacity to function.

Religious abuse, in the basic sense, is just a collection of abuses that are excused by religion or a religious tradition. Sometimes bad theology and bad practice lead to abusive behavior. At other times abusive behavior creates bad theology and bad practice to justify itself. Such abuse ranges from Christians using Scripture to justify slavery to religious leaders

---

[21] Ibid., 39.
[22] Ruth Duck, "Hospitality to Victims," ch. 9 of Andrew Sung Park and Susan Nelson, *The Other Side of Sin,* 167.
[23] John and Paula Sandford, *Healing the Wounded Spirit,* 458–59.
[24] Ibid., 79–80.

manipulating followers for their own self-aggrandizement, or using their positions of trust and authority to sexually prey on minors and others.

The special crime in this abuse is that it blasphemes God and His character. It makes those it affects fear or utterly reject Him, or it puts them in a kind of soul slumber that is seemingly immune to love and relationship.

The ignorance or simple inattention of the Church toward the sinned against prolongs this wounding. One might even extend the umbrella of religious abuse to the Church's sins of omission—the ways in which it has ignored and even harmed those within it who need and seek healing. In the dedication of his book *Why Do Christians Shoot Their Wounded?* Dwight Carlson wrote these telling words:

> There are legions of God-fearing Christians who—to the best of their ability—are walking according to the Scriptures and yet are suffering from emotional symptoms. Many of them have been judged for their condition and given half-truths and clichés by well-meaning but ill-informed fellow believers. To these wounded saints I dedicate this book.[25]

The challenge of religious abuse, and healing for it, is thus both for those who have been disrespected, demeaned, and mistreated by others in the Church, and for those whose wounds have been ignored or denied. Both hurt.

What is the nature of healing, given the wide variety of woundedness stemming from all kinds of abuse? While God is able to heal any kind of infirmity, today the ministry of God's healing by people tends to be narrow in its focus; that is, a given healing ministry will usually specialize in a certain kind of healing—physical, emotional, mental, and so on, and perhaps in an even narrower subcategory.[26] There are several primary foci of such work, among them abuse (physical, sexual, religious); bodily disease, deformity, and injury; sin and forgiveness; and unresolved anger toward God and people.[27]

Note, however, that while a given healing ministry may limit itself to one of these areas, during its work healing often occurs that is outside the bounds of its customary focus. While those who do healing prayer may limit their specialty, God will often respond broadly. For example, the connection between unresolved anger, disturbed bodily functioning, and

---

[25] Dwight L. Carlson, *Why Do Christians Shoot Their Wounded?*, n.p.
[26] Many ministries today look back with appreciation at the work of Agnes Sanford, one of the great illuminators of healing ministry from the last century. For years they have quoted her groundbreaking work *The Healing Light*, which addressed many kinds of healing and looked at the range of areas of healing. However, it has only been in more recent years that some of the finer distinctions among healings have begun to be drawn.
[27] These various categories also apply to wounding that is seemingly without cause (that is, accidental).

82

healing of memories is common in the experience of healing ministries.[28] It should not be surprising that when one area begins to be healed, other wounds are exposed and begin to heal as well, even if they had initially seemed unrelated.

These days, emotional or "soul" healing, sometimes called "inner" healing, is the focus of much of the work of healing in the church. One might wonder how this comports with Scripture and the work of Jesus and others, for did they not mostly heal physical maladies like blindness, epilepsy, and crippled limbs? Why then such a focus today on emotional healing? Are we that different from the people of long ago, or are we just caught up in a psychological fad? It's not uncommon for people in healing ministry to ask themselves these questions. Why is so much of their effort directed to "inner" healing of one sort or another, when physical healing would seem to be much more dramatic and offer even more "proof" that there is a God and that He heals supernaturally?

The fact is that physical healing does occur. Many, if not all, who focus on "inner" healing have witnessed profound physical healings as well. But the healing of inner wounds distinguishes itself in that it can affect every part of one's life, productivity, ability to love and be loved, confidence, hope, and much more. That this inner damage and disability can be healed at all is far-reaching and truly miraculous, and God should be honored for His willingness to do it. Those who minister this healing have no need for jealousy, apology, or regret. It is an honor and a privilege.

Emotional and physical needs are often interconnected, though putting too much emphasis on cause/effect relationships can be both bad psychology and bad theology. However, connections frequently reveal themselves. When through prayer a chaplain was dramatically healed of a 30-year-long case of rheumatoid arthritis, the healing not only freed her from pain, but also completely revolutionized her understanding of and feelings for God. In her words:

> I always believed that God was awful.[29] Now I know that he is sweet. It has changed my ministry and my counseling completely, especially to women who have been abused. Now when I tell them God loves them, and wishes to heal them, I know it is true, because I have experienced it myself.[30]

---

[28] See Margarett Anne Schlientz, "A Study on the Decrease of Unresolved Anger Through a Teaching Protocol and Healing Prayer as a Nursing Intervention in Spiritual Care" (Ph.D. diss., University of Pittsburgh, 1981).

[29] She is using *awful* in the sense of definition 2 in the Oxford English Dictionary: "worthy of, or commanding, profound respect or reverential fear."

[30] Private communication to author during his clinical pastoral education training in seminary, circa 1989.

Similarly, *a wound caused by emotional abuse will often manifest as physical pain and disability.* When the emotional abuse is uncovered and healed, the physical symptoms tend to disappear as well. John and Paula Sandford give examples of this kind of dual healing in *The Transformation of the Inner Man*.[31] *The simple reality is that soul and body are not independent of each other.* Injury to one affects the other; healing of one releases healing in the other. Physical healings like those recorded in Scripture and church history do continue to occur today, but healing itself must be understood much more broadly if we are to realize its importance and centrality to human life.

HEALING IN SCRIPTURE AND CHURCH HISTORY

God is not confined to the experiences of history. If there had never been healing in the past and none had been recorded in Scripture, this would hardly prevent the Author of the universe from doing it today for the first time. Some theological quarters propose that such healings have to be from Satan, but the witness of the fruit of healing testifies to its true Source, and it is notable that some who believe that God has ceased to intervene in human lives by supernatural means will readily propose that Satan continues to do so.[32]

Of course, in "discerning the spirits" and in examining supernatural occurrences, one should exercise caution whether or not there is a previous record of similar events in Scripture or church history. But this does not mean that one should avoid seeking God's intervention and healing. Earnest Gentile reflected in this way on the purpose for the book of Acts:

> Luke's record of the early Church purposes less to account for the doings of the Church than to account for the *doings of God in and through the Church*. It shows us what actually happened and how the Church *realized life through the Holy Spirit*. The primitive Church was the prototype for spiritual concepts designed to work *in every generation and society.* (emphasis added)[33]

Is there, then, a historical record of divine healing? Yes, a prodigious one. There is evidence of it in other cultures prior to the writing of Scripture, throughout Scripture, in the intertestamental literature, and in the history of the Church since the time of Jesus. It is an embarrassment of riches.

---

[31] John and Paula Sandford, *The Transformation of the Inner Man*, 1982. See especially chapter 11, "Inner Vows."

[32] For example, in "An Essay on Faith Healing" in 1969, Victor Weyland wrote: "To what conclusion must a Christian come as he stares these facts in the face? Is it not this that this entire healing craze is a trick of the devil to draw people away from God's revealed plan for our Salvation?" www.wls.wels.net/library/Essays/Authors/w/WeylandFaith/WeylandFaith.rtf

[33] Earnest Gentile, *Your Sons and Daughters Shall Prophesy*, 196.

Archaeological artifacts from the predynastic period in Egypt (6000–5000 B.C.) indicate that evil spirits or demons were believed to be the source of both mental and physical illness. Egyptian, Assyrian, and Persian records attest to the laying on of hands for healing during the time of the Pharaohs (5000–1500 B.C.). Over the course of many millennia, these two types of disease have sometimes been separated, with physical disease attributed to natural causes and mental illness to spiritual causes. Sometimes they have been regarded as having the same cause, whether natural or spiritual. Modern medicine is beginning to again regard mental and physical illness as having similar causes, although debate about whether the cause is natural or supernatural persists, with most Western practitioners inclining to the natural explanations.[34]

THE OLD TESTAMENT

The Old Testament[35] constantly reveals God as a God of healing, able to heal and ready to heal, the One "who heals all your diseases" (Psalm 103:3). He is Jehovah-Rapha, "the LORD who heals you" (Exodus 15:26). In the Hebrew understanding of God's sovereignty (explored in Chapter 2), both wounding and healing ultimately come from (or are permitted by) the Lord: "'Now see that I, even I, am He, and there is no God besides Me; I kill and I make alive; I wound and I heal; nor is there any who can deliver from My hand'" (Deut. 32:39). "Come, and let us return to the LORD; for He has torn, but He will heal us; He has stricken, but He will bind us up" (Hosea 6:1).

Similarly, the psalmist declares, "You, who have shown me great and severe troubles, shall revive me again, and bring me up again from the depths of the earth" (Psalm 71:20). There is even witness to the connection between healing and the abuse, despair, and wounding of the soul or body: "He gathers together the outcasts of Israel. He heals the brokenhearted and binds up their wounds" (Psalm 147:2–3). Solomon counsels that devotion to the Lord brings health: "Do not be wise in your own eyes; Fear the LORD and depart from evil. It will be health to your flesh, and strength to your bones" (Prov. 3:7–8). He even teaches that godly counsel brings health: "The tongue of the wise promotes health" (12:18).

Although God is able to heal and does heal, even without request, *the most common testimony of Scripture is that healing comes in response to calling out for it, occasionally by the one needing healing, but more commonly by another on his or her behalf.* Some examples from the Old

---

[34] Harold G. Koenig, Michael E. McCollough, and David B. Larson, *Handbook of Religion and Health*, 25.
[35] Referring not to value, but only to its creation prior to the New Testament.

Testament will serve to illustrate this model, which persists throughout Scripture and in the experience of the Church to the present time. Elijah was given lodging by a woman with a son who became ill and died. In her despair she asked Elijah, who she knew to be a man of God, why her son had died. Was it to remind her of her sin? Elijah did not reply. Instead, he asked for her son and carried him up to his bed. He then cried out in complaint:

> "O LORD my God, have You also brought tragedy on the widow with whom I lodge, by killing her son?" And he stretched himself out on the child three times, and cried out to the LORD and said, "O LORD my God, I pray, let this child's soul come back to him." Then the LORD heard the voice of Elijah; and the soul of the child came back to him, and he revived. And Elijah took the child and brought him down from the upper room into the house, and gave him to his mother. And Elijah said, "See, your son lives." Then the woman said to Elijah, "Now by this I know that you are a man of God, and that the word of the LORD in your mouth is the truth." (1 Kings 17:20–24)

In this, God's word is affirmed, God is affirmed, His messenger is affirmed, and a son who has died is healed. There is no assent here to the idea that God caused the death as punishment for the mother's sin (Jesus refutes a similar idea in John 9:2–3), but God's willingness to heal is revealed.

Naaman, the commander of the Syrian army, went to Israel to be cured of leprosy. He expected to be healed in a certain way, and when Elijah's disciple Elisha told him what he had to do, he was defiant and went off in a rage. Then when he finally relented and did what the Lord had instructed him to do through Elisha—dipping in the Jordan seven times—he was utterly healed (2 Kings 5:1–15).

The Israelites "cried out to the LORD in their trouble, and He saved them out of their distresses. He sent His word and healed them, and delivered them from their destructions" (Psalm 107:19–20). "Have mercy on me, O LORD, for I am weak," David cried out. "O LORD, heal me, for my bones are troubled" (Ps. 6:2). The Lord heard and healed him: "O LORD my God, I cried out to You, and You healed me" (Ps. 30:2).

David also recognized that sin can cause disease and how this can separate sinners from those they love:

> There is no soundness in my flesh because of Your anger, nor any health in my bones because of my sin. For my iniquities have gone over my head; like a heavy burden they are too heavy for me. My wounds are foul and festering because of my foolishness. I am troubled, I am bowed down greatly; I go mourning all the day long. For my loins are full of inflammation, and there is no soundness in my flesh. I am feeble and

severely broken; I groan because of the turmoil of my heart. Lord, all my desire is before You; and my sighing is not hidden from You. My heart pants, my strength fails me; as for the light of my eyes, it also has gone from me. My loved ones and my friends stand aloof from my plague, and my relatives stand afar off. (Psalm 38:3–11)

Psalm 119, an extraordinary paean of praise to God's Word, connects love of His revelation to well-being:

> My soul clings to the dust; revive me according to Your word. I have declared my ways, and You answered me; teach me Your statutes. Make me understand the way of Your precepts; so shall I meditate on Your wonderful works. My soul melts from heaviness; strengthen me according to Your word. (vv. 25–28)

Scripture recognizes the healing power of love and kindness: "Pleasant words are as a honeycomb, sweetness to the soul and health to the bones" (Proverbs 16:24). It also acknowledges God as Healer, though we do not realize it:

> I taught Ephraim to walk, taking them by their arms; but they did not know that I healed them. I drew them with gentle cords, with bands of love, and I was to them as those who take the yoke from their neck. I stooped and fed them. (Hosea 11:3–4)

The prophet Isaiah is a source of extraordinary insight into disease and healing. In Isaiah 58, he exposes the hearts of those who pretend to fast to please God, but instead structure their fasts to please themselves: "In fact, in the day of your fast you find pleasure, and exploit all your laborers. Indeed you fast for strife and debate, and to strike with the fist of wickedness" (vv. 3–4).

To God, a true fast is not refraining from eating food or wearing sackcloth and ashes, but treating others with godly love:

> Is this not the fast that I have chosen: to loose the bonds of wickedness, to undo the heavy burdens, to let the oppressed go free, and that you break every yoke? Is it not to share your bread with the hungry, and that you bring to your house the poor who are cast out; when you see the naked, that you cover him, and not hide yourself from your own flesh? (Isaiah 58:6–7)

Isaiah describes the consequences of a true fast:

> Then your light shall break forth like the morning, Your healing shall spring forth speedily, and your righteousness shall go before you; the glory of the Lord shall be your rear guard. Then you shall call, and the Lord will answer; you shall cry, and He will say, "Here I am."…

> If you extend your soul to the hungry and satisfy the afflicted soul, then your light shall dawn in the darkness, and your darkness shall be as the noonday.
>
> The Lord will guide you continually, and satisfy your soul in drought, and strengthen your bones; You shall be like a watered garden, and like a spring of water, whose waters do not fail. (vv. 8–11)

The promise for those who heal and care for others is their own strengthening, healing, and a provision that flows like a spring of water. Isaiah 58 goes on to describe the extraordinarily deep and profound relationship the Lord grants His followers when they "fast" by treating others with godly love.

Isaiah is also a source of prophecies about the coming Messiah, and they include much about healing and suffering. First, by willingly taking upon Himself the wounding of the people, the Messiah brings healing:

> Surely He has borne our griefs and carried our sorrows; yet we esteemed Him stricken, smitten by God, and afflicted. But He was wounded for our transgressions, He was bruised for our iniquities; the chastisement for our peace was upon Him, and by His stripes we are healed. (Isaiah 53:4–5)

In the voice of the Messiah to come, Isaiah also proclaims God's desire to heal by His Spirit:

> The Spirit of the Lord GOD is upon me, because the LORD has anointed me to preach good tidings to the poor; He has sent me to heal the brokenhearted, to proclaim liberty to the captives, and the opening of the prison to those who are bound. (Isaiah 61:1)

These words, which Jesus quotes in Luke 4, are meant to be understood broadly: The word *captivity* can describe not only physical confinement, but also demonic oppression, abuse and psychological burden. It is a common reality in healing ministries that Jesus does indeed free people bound in these ways.

Jeremiah, in the midst of attacks on his character and prophecies, appeals to God in his affliction, "Heal me, O LORD, and I shall be healed" (Jeremiah 17:14). Later, after the people have gone into exile as he predicted, Jeremiah prophesies their return, restoration, and healing:

> "All those who devour you shall be devoured; and all your adversaries, every one of them, shall go into captivity; those who plunder you shall become plunder, and all who prey upon you I will make a prey. For I will restore health to you and heal you of your wounds," says the LORD,

"Because they called you an outcast saying: 'This is Zion; No one seeks her.'" (Jer. 30:16–17)

He reinforces this, saying, "Behold, I will bring it health and healing; I will heal them and reveal to them the abundance of peace and truth, and I will cause the captives of Judah and the captives of Israel to return, and will rebuild those places as at the first." (Jeremiah 33:6–7)

Jeremiah depicts a people who refuse the Lord's entreaties to turn from their wickedness, suffer exile and oppression for their intransigence, and then are healed by God. This pattern is also seen in Psalm 85:

> Will You be angry with us forever? Will You prolong Your anger to all generations? Will You not revive us again, that Your people may rejoice in You? Show us Your mercy, LORD, and grant us Your salvation. (85:5–7)

And in Isaiah:

> Thus says the High and Lofty One Who inhabits eternity, whose name is Holy: "I dwell in the high and holy place, with him who has a contrite and humble spirit, to revive the spirit of the humble, and to revive the heart of the contrite ones." (57:15)

The prophet Ezekiel assumes that those who shepherd God's people will care for them, and when they fail in this, he strongly condemns them:

> Thus says the Lord GOD to the shepherds: "Woe to the shepherds of Israel who feed themselves. Should not the shepherds feed the flocks? You eat the fat and clothe yourselves with the wool; you slaughter the fatlings, but you do not feed the flock. The weak you have not strengthened, nor have you healed those who were sick, nor bound up the broken, nor brought back what was driven away, nor sought what was lost; but with force and cruelty you have ruled them." (Ezek. 34:2–4)

God then says He will Himself serve and heal those who have been abused and that He will destroy the abusers: "I will seek what was lost and bring back what was driven away, bind up the broken and strengthen what was sick; but I will destroy the fat and the strong, and feed them in judgment" (v. 16).

In His response, God clearly distinguishes between those who scoff at God and those who fear Him:

> "For behold, the day is coming, burning like an oven, and all the proud, yes, all who do wickedly will be stubble. And the day which is coming shall burn them up," says the LORD of hosts, "that will leave them neither root nor branch. But to you who fear My name the Sun of Righteousness shall arise with healing in His wings; and you shall go out and grow fat like stall-fed calves. You shall trample the wicked, for they shall be ashes

under the soles of your feet on the day that I do this," says the LORD of hosts. (Malachi 4:1–3)

THE APOCRYPHA

Like Jerome, the first translator of the Bible, most Protestants believe the Apocrypha does not rise to the level of inspiration required to be included in the canon of Scripture.[36] Still, this intertestamental literature represents the voice of the Jewish people in the centuries between the close of the Old Testament and the beginning of the New Testament. As a bridge between the two Testaments, it reveals the thinking, theology and culture of the Jewish people during this important and tumultuous period. It is thus valuable to hear what it has to say about healing.

In the book of Tobit, two people are in need of healing. Tobit is a righteous man, faithful to God and the Law, who has been blinded by the droppings of sparrows. Sarah is a woman who has been unjustly accused of killing her seven husbands, when in fact a demon, Asmodeus, killed them all before any of the marriages were consummated.

Sarah, who wants to die to escape her unfair reproach, prays:

> Blessed are you, merciful God. Blessed is your name forever; let all your works praise you forever. And now, Lord, I turn my face to you, and raise my eyes toward you. Command that I be released from the earth and not listen to such reproaches any more. (Tobit 3:11–13)[37]

Tobit also prays, and "at that very moment, the prayers of both of them were heard in the glorious presence of God" (Tobit 3:16), and He sent an angel to heal them:

> So Raphael was sent to heal both of them: Tobit, by removing the white films from his eyes, so that he might see God's light with his eyes; and Sarah, daughter of Raguel, by giving her in marriage to Tobias son of Tobit, and by setting her free from the wicked demon Asmodeus. (Tobit 3:17)

This passage is remarkable in several respects, including Sarah's guileless prayer, which brings healing, the naming of a demon and the delivery from him, and the working of healing by the agency of an angel named only in the book of Tobit and whose name, Raphael, means healing—as in Jehovah-Rapha.

The Wisdom of Solomon is often attributed to King Solomon, and though not considered by many to be in the canon of Scripture, it nevertheless

---

[36] It is actually a bit more complex than this. Some books are considered canonical by some Protestants but not by Roman Catholics. In other cases this judgment is reversed. These judgments, however, will not be reviewed here.

[37] Citations from the Apocrypha are from the New Revised Standard Version.

speaks powerfully and wisely about what can and cannot give strength or heal:

> Miserable, with their hopes set on dead things, are those who give the name "gods" to the works of human hands, gold and silver fashioned with skill, and likenesses of animals, or a useless stone, the work of an ancient hand. ... When he prays about possessions and his marriage and children, he is not ashamed to address a lifeless thing. *For health he appeals to a thing that is weak;* for life he prays to a thing that is dead; for aid he entreats a thing that is utterly inexperienced; for a prosperous journey, a thing that cannot take a step; for money-making and work and success with his hands he asks strength of a thing whose hands have no strength. (Wisdom 13:10, 17–19, emphasis added)

Is this not an extraordinary piece of insight and wisdom about our foolish dependence on the works of our own hands as a source of life and healing? To be clear, this is not a criticism of useful implements or medicine, but of amulets and idols and superstitious totems, which we imagine are imbued with power but are really just fashioned pieces of wood, stone, and metal and are without intelligence or will.

Sirach offers many insights about health and healing. He recognizes the beneficial effects of a right relationship with God: "The fear of the Lord is the crown of wisdom, making peace and perfect health to flourish" (1:18).[38] He also acknowledges that sin can block healing: "When calamity befalls the proud, there is no healing, for an evil plant has taken root in him" (3:28). In the same way, he realizes that the refusal to extend forgiveness can keep us from receiving it from the Lord and being healed:

> Forgive your neighbor the wrong he has done, and then your sins will be pardoned when you pray. Does anyone harbor anger against another, and expect healing from the Lord? If one has no mercy toward another like himself, can he then seek pardon for his own sins? (Sirach 28:2–4)

Many books in recent years have examined the beneficial effects of laughter, as well as the bodily harm done by anger, jealousy, and anxiety. These themes, too, are present in Sirach: "A joyful heart is life itself, and rejoicing lengthens one's life span.... Jealousy and anger shorten life, and anxiety brings on premature old age" (30:22, 24).

Finally, Sirach counsels that physicians are to be sought and honored. Rather than claiming that doctors are at odds with divine healing, or that

---

[38] Here, as in the Old Testament, the fear of the Lord refers to reverential awe, not the kind of fear that an armed robber or rapist might engender.

going to them somehow dishonors God or causes Him to not act, Sirach includes physicians, as well as medicine from pharmacists, as means of God's healing:

> Honor physicians for their services, for the Lord created them; for their gift of healing comes from the Most High, and they are rewarded by the king. The skill of physicians makes them distinguished, and in the presence of the great they are admired. The Lord created medicines out of the earth, and the sensible will not despise them. Was not water made sweet with a tree in order that its power might be known? And he gave skill to human beings that he might be glorified in his marvelous works. By them the physician heals and takes away pain; the pharmacist makes a mixture from them. God's works will never be finished; and from him health spreads over all the earth. My child, when you are ill, do not delay, but pray to the Lord, and he will heal you. (38:1–10)

Note that Sirach's focus is on doctors who pray. He also observes that *unconfessed sin can be a source of illness and that people who persist in their sin will defy physicians much as they defy God:*

> Give up your faults and direct your hands rightly, and cleanse your heart from all sin. Then give the physician his place, for the Lord created him; do not let him leave you, for you need him. There may come a time when recovery lies in the hands of physicians, for they too pray to the Lord that he grant them success in diagnosis and in healing, for the sake of preserving life. He who sins against his Maker, will be defiant toward the physician. (Sirach 38:12–15)

Clearly, Scripture's themes about healing also appear in the intertestamental literature.

THE NEW TESTAMENT

The intention of God to bring healing through the Messiah and His followers is found early in the New Testament text:

> "And she will bring forth a Son, and you shall call His name JESUS, for He will save His people from their sins." So all this was done that it might be fulfilled which was spoken by the Lord through the prophet, saying: "Behold, the virgin shall be with child, and bear a Son, and they shall call His name Immanuel," which is translated, "God with us." (Matt. 1:21–23)

This passage declares that "God saves," the literal meaning of "Jesus," and that "God is with us," the literal meaning of "Immanuel." Though it does not speak explicitly of healing, it is an indication of God's intentions toward us. Those intentions, along with their effects, are quickly proven out in chapter 4:

Jesus went about all Galilee, teaching in their synagogues, preaching the gospel of the kingdom, and healing all kinds of sickness and all kinds of disease among the people. Then His fame went throughout all Syria; and they brought to Him all sick people who were afflicted with various diseases and torments, and those who were demon-possessed, epileptics, and paralytics; and He healed them. Great multitudes followed Him—from Galilee, and from Decapolis, Jerusalem, Judea, and beyond the Jordan. (Matt. 4:23–25)

Matthew 8:16–17 directly links the actions of Jesus with Isaiah's prophecies about the coming Messiah: "He cast out the spirits with a word, and healed all who were sick, that it might be fulfilled which was spoken by Isaiah the prophet, saying: 'He Himself took our infirmities and bore our sicknesses.'" (In Isaiah 53:4, the two nouns are חֱלִי, *choliy* and מַכְאֹב, *mak'ob.* The former means sickness, disease or grief; the latter means sorrow, pain or grief, both physical and mental.)

As He proclaimed the good news of the Kingdom and healed people in need, Jesus extended His ministry beyond Himself:

Jesus went about all the cities and villages, teaching in their synagogues, preaching the gospel of the kingdom, and healing every sickness and every disease among the people. But when He saw the multitudes, He was moved with compassion for them, because they were weary and scattered, like sheep having no shepherd. Then He said to His disciples, "The harvest truly is plentiful, but the laborers are few. Therefore pray the Lord of the harvest to send out laborers into His harvest." (Matt. 9:35–38)

That is, Jesus instructed His disciples to pray for more laborers (more disciples, more workers for the Kingdom) and then sent them, initially, to the "lost sheep of the house of Israel" (Matthew 10:6) with these instructions: "As you go, preach, saying, 'The kingdom of heaven is at hand.' Heal the sick, cleanse the lepers, raise the dead, cast out demons. Freely you have received, freely give" (Matt. 10:7–8).

"The kingdom of heaven is at hand" is often interpreted to mean "coming soon," but it was generally understood to mean "close by" in distance, not time. It also echoes a root word (ἐγγίζω, *eggizo*) that refers to making disciples. That is, Immanuel, God with us—the kingdom of heaven right here—is naturally followed by healing. This is why in healing prayer we invite God's presence.

In Matthew 12 there is a more extended revelation of the connection between God's presence and healing. The Pharisees have accused Jesus and

His disciples of violating the Sabbath by plucking and eating heads of grain. After pointing out that David and his men ate bread from the temple on the Sabbath, Jesus says:

> I say to you that in this place there is One greater than the temple. But if you had known what this means, "I desire mercy and not sacrifice," you would not have condemned the guiltless. For the Son of Man is Lord even of the Sabbath. (Matthew 12:6–8)

In a similar passage in Mark, Jesus says, "The Sabbath was made for man, and not man for the Sabbath. Therefore the Son of Man is also Lord of the Sabbath" (2:27–28). In these two passages Jesus says something about Himself that the Pharisees considered blasphemous.[39] He claims that He is both Lord of the Sabbath and greater than the temple. And then He proceeds to demonstrate what He has just asserted:

> Now when He had departed from there, He went into their synagogue. And behold, there was a man who had a withered hand. And they asked Him, saying, "Is it lawful to heal on the Sabbath?"—that they might accuse Him. Then He said to them, "What man is there among you who has one sheep, and if it falls into a pit on the Sabbath, will not lay hold of it and lift it out? Of how much more value then is a man than a sheep? Therefore it is lawful to do good on the Sabbath." Then He said to the man, "Stretch out your hand." And he stretched it out, and it was restored as whole as the other. Then the Pharisees went out and plotted against Him, how they might destroy Him. (Matt. 12:9–14)

The Pharisees understood Jesus' claim quite well, but they ignored the proof of it and began plotting His destruction. Matthew continues:

> But when Jesus knew it, He withdrew from there. And great multitudes followed Him, and He healed them all. Yet He warned them not to make Him known, that it might be fulfilled which was spoken by Isaiah the prophet, saying: "Behold. My Servant whom I have chosen, My Beloved in whom My soul is well pleased. I will put My Spirit upon Him, and He will declare justice to the Gentiles. He will not quarrel nor cry out, nor will anyone hear His voice in the streets. A bruised reed He will not break, and smoking flax He will not quench, till He sends forth justice to victory; and in His name Gentiles will trust [Isaiah 42:1–4]." (Matt. 12:15–21)[40]

The Holy Spirit was present upon Jesus as, with great gentleness, He continued to declare benefits of God's kingdom and heal those who followed Him:

---

[39] This claim, and the response to it, is similar to the one Jesus makes in Luke 5 and Mark 2.
[40] In the Greek, the word *Gentiles* (εθνος, *ethnos)* means people of all races, as distinct from the Jews.

Great multitudes came to Him, having with them the lame, blind, mute, maimed, and many others; and they laid them down at Jesus' feet, and He healed them. So the multitude marveled when they saw the mute speaking, the maimed made whole, the lame walking, and the blind seeing; and they glorified the God of Israel. (Matt. 15:30–31)

In their running debate with Jesus, the Pharisees later accused Him of casting out demons by the power of "Beelzebub, the ruler of the demons" (Matt. 12:24). Refuting this accusation as a logical impossibility, Jesus again says that the healing is by the Holy Spirit and that the kingdom of God is near at hand: "If I cast out demons by the Spirit of God," He says, "surely the kingdom of God has come upon you" (v. 28).

Further, He warns that such healing work is not to be attributed to Satan:

Therefore I say to you, every sin and blasphemy will be forgiven men, but the blasphemy against the Spirit will not be forgiven men. Anyone who speaks a word against the Son of Man, it will be forgiven him; but whoever speaks against the Holy Spirit, it will not be forgiven him, either in this age or in the age to come. (Matthew 12:31–32)

These words should be a great caution to those present-day Christians who, believing miracles ceased after the apostolic age, claim that healing in response to prayer is from Satan.

When we read the record of Jesus healing people, it often says that He healed "all"—yet there were times when He did not heal, as when He visited Nazareth and was ridiculed by the residents there:

Jesus said to them, "A prophet is not without honor except in his own country, among his own relatives, and in his own house." Now He could do no mighty work there, except that He laid His hands on a few sick people and healed them. And He marveled because of their unbelief. (Mark 6:4–6)

This recalls Naaman's defiance toward Elisha, as well as the defiance of the ill toward God and the physician as noted in Sirach. Jesus healed a few people in Nazareth but could not do mighty works there, apparently because of the people's unbelief.

In Luke 4, Jesus quotes from Isaiah 61 to proclaim that the Spirit is upon Him and that He has been anointed to preach to the poor, heal the brokenhearted, set captives free, give sight to the blind, and release the oppressed. Clearly, His healings extend far beyond simple physical restoration. All these healings are part of the ministry of Jesus through His body, the Church. Jesus presented it this way:

Believe Me that I am in the Father and the Father in Me, or else believe Me for the sake of the works themselves. Most assuredly, I say to you, he who believes in Me, the works that I do he will do also; and greater works than these he will do, because I go to My Father. And whatever you ask in My name, that I will do, that the Father may be glorified in the Son. If you ask anything in My name, I will do it. If you love Me, keep My commandments. And I will pray the Father, and He will give you another Helper, that He may abide with you forever—the Spirit of truth, whom the world cannot receive, because it neither sees Him nor knows Him; but you know Him, for He dwells with you and will be in you. I will not leave you orphans; I will come to you. A little while longer and the world will see Me no more, but you will see Me. Because I live, you will live also. At that day you will know that I am in My Father, and you in Me, and I in you. He who has My commandments and keeps them, it is he who loves Me. And he who loves Me will be loved by My Father, and I will love him and manifest Myself to him. (John 14:11–21)

Jesus gave the authority to do these works first to the Twelve, and then to the Seventy (Luke 10:1, 17), and then to the entire body of Christ—to all who believe. The *"great commission"* of Matt. 28:19 *specifies the authority* Jesus gave to make new disciples throughout the world: "In the name of the Father and of the Son and of the Holy Spirit" is *legal terminology* that refers to the *"power of attorney" one person assigns to another.*

Jesus' willingness to heal is evident in all the Gospels, and the balance of the New Testament testifies to God's willingness to heal miraculously through Jesus' followers. Evident throughout is the combination of celebration, accusation and disbelief that accompanied these miracles. At Lystra, when Paul healed a man who had never walked, onlookers thought he and Barnabas were pagan gods (Acts 14:8–12). When Peter did the same thing in the temple, the people were incredulous. "Men of Israel, why do you marvel at this?" Peter asked, "Or why look so intently at us, as though by our own power or godliness we had made this man walk?" (Acts 3:12). Healings accomplished by God through the Body of Christ meet with similar reactions today.

Sometimes God healed through His followers in odd, unexpected ways: "God worked unusual miracles by the hands of Paul, so that even handkerchiefs or aprons were brought from his body to the sick, and the diseases left them and the evil spirits went out of them" (Acts 19:11–12). And people brought their sick into the streets so that when Peter walked by, his shadow would fall on them and heal them (Acts 5:15).

Though Paul had some physical infirmity or disability that God would not heal (the "thorn in the flesh" mentioned in 2 Corinthians 12:7), Paul was healed of a desperate disease of his soul at his conversion. Healing has always been understood to include disease of the soul as well as the body. Augustine refers to this when he says,

> [Paul's conversion] fulfilled in him what was written in the prophet, "I will strike, and I will heal" (Isaiah 19:22). *What God strikes, you see, is that in people which lifts up itself against God.* The surgeon isn't being heartless when he lances the tumor, when he cuts or burns out the suppurating sore. *He's causing pain; he certainly is, but in order to restore health.* It's a horrid business; but if it wasn't, it wouldn't be any use.[41]

Augustine's insight here also applies to many healings today: They often begin with great pain and distress, which then blossoms into profound healing and release.

HEALING IN THE HISTORY OF THE CHRISTIAN CHURCH

Not surprisingly, the record of the Christian church in the area of healing has at times been characterized by its excesses, just as at times it has been characterized by its absence. Such accounts as the resurrection of the dead man whose body touched the bones of Elisha (2 Kings 13:21) and the working of miracles through Paul's handkerchief and Peter's shadow have spawned some superstitions and questionable practices in the Church. In recent years these have included the selling of prayer cloths, holy water, and other objects by several TV ministries, as well as at some Roman Catholic shrines. However, the use of holy objects in healing is not new.

The question of how healing happens through them is seldom directly addressed in the literature, though assumptions about it seem implicit in the descriptions of certain practices. Chief among these is the long-standing belief in the healing power of the Communion bread and wine . Though many Western Protestants and Protestant theologians would, like Zwingli, describe the Communion meal as simply an important "remembrance," the view of the Church for 1100 years was that Communion was much more than that. It was the "real presence" of the body and blood of Jesus and thus had enormous healing power. Theologians who supported this position included Ambrose, Augustine, Chrysostom, Cyril, Justin Martyr, Irenaeus and Tertullian. Both the Roman Catholic and the Eastern Orthodox church still assert this as basic doctrine.

There was essentially no controversy on this point at all until the 9th century, when the nature of the "real presence" was first expounded upon by the theologian Paschasius Radbertus. Then around 1047, one lone monk, Berengarius of Tours, opined that he did not consider the "real presence" to

---

[41] Augustine, "Sermon 77.3," ed. Joseph Lienhard, reprinted in *Ancient Christian Commentary on Scripture: Old Testament*, 3:335–36.

be present. But this idea gained no purchase at all until centuries later, when Calvin, Luther, Zwingli and others began to re-examine the 9th-century debate and Berengarius' opinions.

The Reformers tended to discount the supernatural suppositions of the Roman church and Aquinas, particularly in relation to the Eucharist and the Mass (as in Aquinas' assertion that the bread and wine underwent transubstantiation—change of substance—and became Christ's literal body and blood), and this extended also to a general mistrust of supernatural explanations and assertions. This is not to imply the absence of the mystical: Calvin believed the Holy Spirit was supernaturally involved in Communion, as did Luther, but not by a change in their physical structure. Luther believed in the real presence by "consubstantiation," Calvin by "dynamic" or "virtual" presence. Only Zwingli regarded it as a mere memorial supper.

Modern churches that accept the possibility of the "real presence" understand Communion as a potentially powerful encounter between the living presence of Christ and those coming to the altar, and it is not uncommon to see manifestations of the Holy Spirit present in those encounters.

As in the past, the Roman church today believes the healing presence of Jesus is in the Communion elements. Throughout the centuries it has sent *viaticum*—literally "supply for a journey"—to the sick and dying. This typically consists of consecrated bread dipped in wine and carried, usually by a priest or deacon, in preparation for death to those who are dying, or for healing to those who are too sick to go to church.

Over the centuries, Christians reverenced not only the elements of Communion, but also relics, like pieces of the "true" cross, Jesus' tears, Mary's milk, the bones of saints, and holy shrines such as Lourdes. Such relics and places were thought to contain some deposit of grace or holiness and were often regarded in a magical, superstitious way. Some caution is appropriate, though, in too quickly dismissing all of this as a product of ignorance or superstition, though it might seem so in our modern, "scientific" age, especially given Scripture's accounts of the healing effects of Peter's shadow, Paul's handkerchief, and Elisha's bones.

Protestants especially often confuse Enlightenment epistemology with rigorous theology and tend to dismiss as unreal anything that smacks of the supernatural. Those who admit the possibility that things might happen for other than material causes are often treated with pride and condescension. Others believe that relics are effective but only because of the *placebo* effect. That is, they believe the faith of the ill person in the religious object (or in a simple sugar pill) causes their healing. [42] Still others readily allow that demonic influences can cause supernatural events, but refuse to concede that they could be the product of the Holy Spirit.

Despite dissenting voices and modern skepticism, the history of the Church clearly demonstrates the perseverance of the belief in divine power for healing. The insights of the great luminaries of church history help put this into greater relief.

In the apostolic age, Clement (99 A.D.) spoke of the gifts of the Spirit given to believers—especially the word of knowledge, instruction, and prophecy—as intended to serve "the spiritual brethren."[43] Yet based on Ecclesiastes 3:7, he also cautioned, "At one time it is proper to keep silence, and at another time to speak." He counseled believers to use judgment and caution in exercising their gifts, set down "rules for visits, exorcisms, and how people are to assist the sick, and to walk in all things without offence," and dealt explicitly with the nature and conduct of healing.[44]

In his ninth homily, Clement went into even more detail, including an in-depth discussion of demons and disease and the manner of life required of a healer. "You shall drive out evil spirits and dire demons, with terrible diseases, from others," he said. "And sometimes they will flee from you when you but look on them." He also said, "He who has given himself to God, being faithful, is heard when he only speaks to demons and diseases." [45] None of this was a mystery to Clement or his contemporaries.

In the immediate post-apostolic (or Ante-Nicene) age, Irenaeus (ca.130–200), in arguing against heresy, mentioned prophecy, exorcism, and even resurrection of the dead as contemporary miracles.[46] In *Against Heresies* he said of the works of the Church in his day:

> For some do certainly and truly drive out devils, so that those who have thus been cleansed from evil spirits frequently both believe [in Christ], and join themselves to the Church. Others...see visions, and utter prophetic expressions. Others still, heal the sick by laying their hands upon them, and they are made whole...the dead have even been raised up, and remained among us for many years. ... It is not possible to name the number of gifts

---

[42] Bernie S. Siegel, *Love, Medicine and Miracles*, 35.
[43] Many believe Clement was a coworker of the apostles and possibly even Paul's "fellow laborer" in Philippians 4:3.
[44] Clement, *First Epistle of the Blessed Clement, Disciple of Peter the Apostle,* reprinted in A. Cleveland Cox, *The Ante-Nicene Fathers*, 8:59–60.
[45] Ibid., 277.
[46] Philip Schaff, *History of the Christian Church*, 2:118.

which the Church, [scattered] throughout the whole world, has received from God...[47]

Justin Martyr (30–165) said miraculous cures were commonplace,[48] and Tertullian (ca. 60–260), in presenting the case for Christians, recalled how the clerk of a court, "one of them who was liable to be thrown upon the ground by an evil spirit, was set free from his affliction; as was also the relative of another, and the little boy of a third." He went on to say, "How many men of rank (to say nothing of the common people) have been delivered from devils, and healed of diseases."[49]

Tertullian also asserted that many conversions in his time were the product of "supernatural dreams and visions."[50] This same kind of miraculous conversion through dreams seems to be occurring today in the lives of many Muslims and is even becoming a part of evangelism efforts to reach them.[51]

Origen (185–254) expounded at length on Paul's words in 1 Corinthians 11:30: "For this reason many are weak and sick among you, and many sleep." He pointed out that not all sin led to sickness, but that some certainly did, most particularly "sickness of the soul," which afflicted those who loved money, ambition, boys, and women. Of these, he said that Jesus had compassion and healed them.[52] This is particularly notable because this early commentator explicitly included in the healing work of Jesus nonphysical healings that are also common in the healing work of the Church today, including the healing of "sex addicts" and "homosexuals," the latter of which has caused much resistance and furor in society and in some quarters of the Church.

Origen referred to the "signs and wonders" that were to some degree "still preserved among those who regulate their lives by the precepts of the Gospel."[53] He also taught that God would bring healing "in order to accept toils with delight and not unwillingly."[54]

Gregory Thaumaturgus (213–270) apparently worked countless astonishing miracles. His second name, bestowed by the Church, literally means "worker of miracles." He was even referred to as "a second Moses." He is said to have banished demons, healed disease, moved a large stone, dried up a

[47] Irenaeus, *Against Heresies*, reprinted in A. Cleveland Cox, *The Apostolic Fathers with Justin Martyr and Irenaeus*, 1:409.
[48] Schaff, *History*, 2:118.
[49] Tertullian, *To Scapula*, reprinted in Cox, *The Ante-Nicene Fathers*, 3:107.
[50] Schaff, *History*, 2:118.
[51] Rick Love, *Muslims, Magic and the Kingdom of God*. The website "Who is Isa al Masih?", devoted to Muslims, contains many of these stories. [https://isaalmasih.net]
[52] Origen, *Commentary on Matthew*, book 10:24, in Cox, *Ante-Nicene Fathers*, 9:430.
[53] Origen, *Against Celsus*, in Cox, *Ante-Nicene Fathers*, 4:397.
[54] Origen, *Homilies on Numbers 27:12*, ed. Joseph T. Lienhard, reprinted in *Ancient Christian Commentary on Scripture: Old Testament*, 3:266.

lake and changed the course of a river, all by speaking a word. Incredible as such tales may seem to modern Christians, Gregory has been defended over the years by many worthy commentators, including Cardinal Newman of England (1801–1890), who at one time doubted virtually all post-apostolic miracles.[55] There are numerous older writings about Gregory's miracles, including the *Life and Panegyric of Gregory* by Gregory of Nyssa, the *Historia Miraculorum* by Russinus, *De Spiritu Sacto* by Basil, and an anonymous sixth-century Syriac manuscript.

Since the Nicene and Post-Nicene eras (311–600 A.D.), many churches around the world (primarily Roman Catholic and Orthodox) have venerated reliquaries that are believed to bring healing—bits of bone, blood or other items from saints (including their clothing, furniture, and the instruments of their death), as well as pieces of wood from the "true cross." Philip Schaff's *History of the Christian Church* looks at the development of this practice in the Church and the varying views over time of its legitimacy.

Schaff's quote from Goethe is telling: "The most glorious thing that the mind conceives is always set upon by a throng of more and more foreign matter."[56] That is, when real miracles occur, particularly through unusual means such as relics, we often err by undue adoration, superstition, or exaggeration in our perception of them. That is perhaps why Augustine of Hippo (354–371) railed against the sale of relics, both real and false, even though he, Jerome (340–420) and Ambrose (340–397) all testified to the authenticity of numerous miracles because they themselves had witnessed them.[57]

Augustine, like many other leaders of the Church, did not regard healing to be the sole province of the Church and generally regarded secular medicine favorably. He and others actively encouraged caring for the sick because they saw the practice of medicine as evidence of God's love and compassion for suffering humanity.[58]

During this period (350–370 A.D.), as a direct result of the Christian virtue of charity and its expression in caring for the sick as taught in Matthew 25:36, hospitals for the care of the sick were first conceived and used. Prior to this, the practice of medicine was private and was unavailable to the general population. A hospital specifically for the treatment of the mentally ill was established in Jerusalem in 491, and by the sixth century they were regularly cared for in monasteries, where many monks were trained and worked as physicians. From the fifth

---

[55] Schaff, *History,* 2:800.
[56] Ibid., 3:450.
[57] Ibid., 3:458–61.
[58] Koenig, *The Healing Power of Faith,* 31–33.

through tenth centuries, the practice of medicine was largely done by apprenticeship, but by the twelfth it had moved into medical schools and become a key element in the training of clergy.[59] Both divine healing and the provision of medicine and physicians were regarded as gifts from God.

Church history records more miracles in the fourth century alone than in all the years since the time of the apostles. The Church Fathers sometimes testified to their truthfulness and other times denied that miracles continued to occur.[60] Another insight into healing in the Church is found in a fifth-century letter written by Pope Innocent I (417 A.D.) to Decentius. In setting down the rules of order in the conduct of the life of the Church, he wrote: "It is licit not only for priests, but also for all Christians to anoint with holy oil in (his or) their times of special need."[61]

During the Middle Ages, supernatural dreams and visions were common in monasteries, and some of their founders made decisions based on them. And though many of the accounts of that era would today be considered mere fancy, some of the most reliable writers testify to innumerable miracles.[62]

Hildegard (1098–1179) was one of the so-called monastic prophets whose activities illuminate this period. The abbess of Disebodenberg, Germany, Hildegard experienced and taught about the Holy Spirit and challenged the Church to return to Scripture. A student of nature, she wrote extensive treatises on herbs and was also a worker of miracles. It is said that "scarcely a person came to her without being healed," and St. Bernard of Clairvaux spoke of her revelation of heavenly knowledge through the Holy Spirit.[63]

As the Middle Ages wore on, the belief in the supernatural never waned, though for a time it did focus more on the supernatural acts of Satan and demons than on the miracles of God.[64] (This would be true in our time as well.) Even in England, where the Church seemed endlessly enmeshed in the politics of the kingdom, stories of miraculous healings can readily be found. Perhaps the best-known are those associated with Thomas à Becket (1118–1170), considered by many a hero of the faith. Though his

---

[59] Ibid., 33.

[60] Schaff, *History*, 3:463–64.

[61] Michael Anthony Diebold, "The Letter of Pope Innocent I to Decentius of Gubbio, a Translation and Commentary" (Master of Arts Thesis, Notre Dame University, 1974), 13.

[62] Schaff, *History*, 5:31, fn 2. Schaff cites *Miracles* by Peter the Venerable, *Dialogue of Miracles* by Caesar of Heisterbach, and *Golden Legend* by Jacobus de Voragine as examples of reliable sources after the turn of the first millennium.

[63] Schaff, *History*, 5:372. However, some have expressed doubts about whether they had actually met. See "St. Hildegard," *New Advent Catholic Encyclopedia*, http://www.newadvent.org/cathen/07351a.htm

[64] See, for example, "Demonology and the Dark Arts" in Schaff, *History*, vol. 5, section 136.

murder in the Canterbury cathedral is usually a focus of political history, healing occurred at his tomb. It was said, "The blind see, the deaf hear, the dumb speak, the lame walk, the lepers are cleansed, the devils are cast out, even the dead are raised to life."[65] These miracles were said to have begun the very evening he was murdered.

Much of the Church today, both Protestant and Roman Catholic, derives its theology and spiritual anthropology from the works of Luther, Calvin and Zwingli, either explicitly or implicitly. Though Luther himself often spoke bitterly against reason, the Reformation owed a great deal to the logical and methodical approach to understanding the world that emerged in the 12th and 13th centuries. This empirical approach, probably evidenced most profoundly in Zwingli, continues to influence much of the Protestant church today.[66]

The empirical approach had itself been fueled by the rediscovery of Aristotle's works and the theology of Thomas Aquinas, much of which was based on Aristotle. Going even further, the Reformers tended to discount the supernatural suppositions of the Roman church and Aquinas, particularly in relation to the Eucharist and the Mass, and this extended to a general mistrust of supernatural explanations for healing and miracles. Their writings, though deeply spiritual, tended to be cogent arguments for theological positions, rather than reports of the supernatural acts of God. Even so, supernatural healings continued, including that of Melanchthon by Luther himself.[67]

Since the Reformation, there have been many exceptions to this more "rational" approach to the Christian life. Certainly the Pentecostal revival of the early twentieth century was notable for its focus on the supernatural, but it is only one of many examples of the break with the empirical approach that have occurred regularly since the Reformation. Again and again over the centuries, there has been a rediscovery of God's power to heal.[68]

Even prior to the rise of Pentecostalism, which is based on the implicit belief that the Holy Spirit is still active in the lives of believers in all the gifts of the Spirit, many ministries taught that the gospel of Jesus Christ was intended not just for the redemption of sinners, but also for the healing of infirmities. Many of these ministries, in turn, were rooted in the work of John and Charles Wesley during the eighteenth century.

---

[65] Schaff, *History*, 5:145.
[66] Ibid., 7:32. For cogent quotes from Luther, see 7:31, footnote.
[67] Will Oursler, *The Healing Power of Faith*, 44–45.
[68] The break was not complete, of course. An approach can be nonempirical (in the sense used here) and yet rest on scientific analyses and reports of supernatural occurrences.

John Wesley (1703–1791), who preached widely during his day, focused on repentance, salvation and holiness. While his statistics are stunning—225,000 miles traveled on horseback, 40,000 sermons preached—perhaps even more so is the work of the Holy Spirit when he preached. Phenomena that had been seen among the Quakers a century earlier became so common in his meetings that he worried when they did not appear. Francis MacNutt describes one of Wesley's meetings:

> He was preaching at Bristol, to people who cried as in the agonies of death, who were struck to the ground and lay there groaning, who were released (so it seemed) with a visible struggle then and there from the power of the devil.[69]

As in modern times, many religious people objected to this work. One bishop said that he considered it his life's work to "extirpate" the work of Methodism. Even Wesley's close associate George Whitefield confronted Wesley about his methods. Yet the day after the confrontation, Whitefield was himself rebuked by the Holy Spirit during his own preaching.

> "Four persons sunk down close to him, almost in the same moment. One of them lay without sense or motion. A second trembled exceedingly. The third had strong convulsions, but made no noise, unless by groans. The fourth, equally convulsed, called upon God, with strong cries and tears." Wesley's response to Whitefield was: "I trust we shall all suffer God to carry on his own work in the way that pleaseth him."[70]

A century later, Charles Cullis, a pioneer in the healing movements of the nineteenth century, said, "Some are tempted to temporize, and tone down the Gospel to please men on whom they think themselves dependent." Yet, "perfect reliance on Christ is impossible so long as you are cherishing your good name as a treasure more precious than his glory."[71]

In the mid-nineteenth century, Ethan Allen, adopting the Methodists' focus on holiness, tied together sin and disease as cause and effect.[72] One of the outcomes of Allen's work was a surge in healing ministries in "homes," where the ill were taken for care and healing prayer. In some ways this echoed the invention of hospitals by Christians who were following the teaching of Jesus in Matthew 25:36.[73]

Elizabeth and Edward Mix not only traveled widely with a successful healing ministry, but also argued persuasively that the miraculous gifts of

---

[69] Francis MacNutt, *Overcome by the Spirit*, 99.
[70] Ibid., 104. Quoted from Wesley's journal.
[71] Charles Cullis, "Let Go and Trust," tract published by Willard Tract Depository, n.d, copied in chapter 15 of Daniel Steele, *Milestone Papers*.
[72] Paul Gale Chappell, "The Divine Healing Movement in America" (Ph.D. diss., Drew University, 1983), 87–88.
[73] "I was sick and you visited Me"—literally, "cared for" or "looked after."

the Spirit had not ended with the close of the apostolic age.[74] Their ministry, like Ethan Allen's before them, spawned many other healers and healing ministries, as well as advocates and defenders like Carrie Judd Montgomery, an invalid healed through Mix's ministry.[75]

A. B. Simpson, a Presbyterian who later founded the Christian and Missionary Alliance, experienced an instantaneous healing through the ministry of Charles Cullis and later contributed to both the growth of healing ministry and world missions.[76] Much of this work is largely unknown to healing ministries begun in the last fifty years, and it is not even cited in current works.

In the early twentieth century, perhaps in response to the Christian Science movement and impelled by the Pentecostal movement's openness to the miraculous, any number of healing ministries were founded within traditional denominations. In 1905 both the Guild of Health in England and the seminal Emmanuel Movement in America endeavored to draw together ministers and doctors to focus both spiritually and physically on the curing of disease. Shortly thereafter, this was followed by the Guild of St. Raphael, an Anglican organization aimed at reestablishing "spiritual means for the healing of the sick." Many others were subsequently formed in the nineteenth century, including the Guild of Pastoral Psychology, the Divine Healing Mission, the Friends' Spiritual Healing Fellowship, the Methodist Society for Medical and Pastoral Practice, and the Churches' Council of Healing.[77]

Of particular interest is the Milton Abbey, which was called a "Home for the Spiritual Treatment of Nervous Suffering."[78] Founded by Rev. John Maillard, it welcomed individuals in psychological distress and had more than 9000 prayer ministers divided into teams. Maillard's work anticipated the contemporary resurgence of healing ministries that once again see body, mind and spirit as an integrated and mutually dependent whole.

In 1950, a study was begun of numerous reports of miracle healings that were occurring across denominational lines. A survey conducted by the head of the Department of Pastoral Services of the National Council of

---

[74] Chappell, "The Divine Healing Movement in America," 93–98.
[75] Joyce Lee and Glenn Gohr, "Women in the Pentecostal Movement," *Enrichment Journal: A Journal for Pentecostal Ministry*
http://www.ag.org/enrichmentjournal/199904/060_women.cfm
[76] Vinson Synan, *The Twentieth-Century Pentecostal Explosion: The Exciting Growth of Pentecostal Churches and Charismatic Renewal Movements*, 162–63; Chappell, "The Divine Healing Movement in America," 251.
[77] Leslie D. Weatherhead, *Psychology, Religion and Healing*, 218–22 and ch. 6.
[78] Ibid., 222.

Churches found that of the 460 ministers who replied to the survey, 160 reported healings. The means of healing were listed as follows, in order of rank:[79]

prayer	117
assurance of forgiveness	57
affirmation	49
laying on of hands	37
anointing	26
other methods	24
rituals	18

It is not clear whether this is a measure of effectiveness, or simply preference for one method or another, and since these total more than twice 160, more than one method was used in many instances.

Some of the most powerful reports of this period reflect the work of the Holy Spirit not in what others might categorize specifically as "healing," but in instances where lives were profoundly changed and redirected. This is healing of the soul, to be sure, and so should not be dismissed.

HEALING IN MORE-RECENT MINISTRIES

One brief but substantive theological work on the subject of healing is T. J. McCrossan's *Bodily Healing and the Atonement*.[80] His work was one of the early influences on the ministry of Kenneth Hagin, whose evangelistic healing services and Rhema Bible Training Center impacted generations of "Word of Faith" churches and pastors.

While not all writers on healing would agree with McCrossan that the healing work of Jesus was in the Atonement or that the role of the believer today is to "appropriate it" by faith, he argues compellingly that both the New and Old Testaments unrelentingly portray God as healer, and he demonstrates by a careful exegesis of the biblical texts that the atoning work of Jesus on the cross was both for redemption from sin and for healing from disease.

Many large healing ministries were founded in the twentieth century, among them Kenneth Hagin, Benny Hinn, Kathryn Kuhlman, Aimee Semple McPherson, William Branham, Charles and Francis Hunter, Ed Smith, Francis and Judith MacNutt, Rita Bennett, John Wimber, John Arnott, Rodney Howard Brown, Randy Clark, Steve Hill, Leanne Payne, Oral and Richard Roberts, Smith Wigglesworth, and Agnes Sanford.

---

[79] Oursler, *The Healing Power of Faith*, 131.
[80] T. J. McCrossan, *Bodily Healing and the Atonement*.

Only a few of these ministries focused any substantive writing on the subject of "how to pray for healing," Rita Bennett and Ed Smith being notable exceptions. Most instead focused on the ministry of healing itself, rather than on training. Some had magazines and other publications, and some were written about by others (often critically), but few produced enduring books on the theology and practical teaching of healing. Donnie Eddings says that the consequence of this is both fear and ignorance, which must be reduced by "education and training [that] unlock the bondage of fear from God's people."[81]

Though these large healing ministries have helped make the public open to healing, the ministry of healing also needs to take place in local churches across the nation and world, where millions gather for worship every week. The challenge then is to teach the local body of Christ how to invite and participate in healing. Simply watching healing occur on TV or attending great crusades will not establish it in the local church.

Two examples of healers who focus on training others to heal are Rita Bennett and Ed Smith.[82] Rita Bennett has not only personally trained thousands, but she has also trained dozens of trainers, who have trained thousands more in a series of highly detailed trainings called the "Emotionally Free Course," based on her book *You Can Be Emotionally Free*.[83]

Ed Smith has trained thousands of local believers in healing prayer through the ministry of "God's light," which can illumine and heal people as the Holy Spirit is invited into areas of darkness in them. Smith is careful to distinguish this ministry from counseling, defining it instead as discovering spiritual bondage by the light of God, receiving the truth that overcomes the lie that caused the bondage, and allowing the Lord to bless the one healed. While not nearly as well-known as some of the more visible "healers," Smith's work is comprehensive and foundational. His terminology is not identical to other authors who teach healing prayer, but the basic theological underpinnings are the same.[84]

Other contemporary authors include Frank and Ida Mae Hammond, whose *Pigs in the Parlor* has sold over a million copies worldwide.[85]

---

[81] Donnie Rose Eddings, "A Seminar Presenting the Team Approach to Prayer for the Psychological, Spiritual, and Physical Healing of People in Foursquare Churches in Southern California" (D.Min. Applied Research Project, Oral Roberts University, 1997), 11.
[82] Francis and Judith MacNutt also do some training as part of their healing-prayer sessions.
[83] Rita Bennett, *You Can Be Emotionally Free*.
[84] Ed M. Smith, *Beyond Tolerable Recovery*, 118. Smith calls this "theophostic ministry."
[85] Frank and Ida Mae Hammond, *Pigs in the Parlor*.

Contrast this book, which focuses so intensely on demonic oppression that demons seem to be behind every doorpost, with Francis and Judith MacNutt's *Healing* and *Deliverance from Evil Spirits,* also immensely popular, which takes a simpler and substantially more seasoned approach to both healing and deliverance.[86]

Leanne Payne had a long ministry primarily but not exclusively to the sexually broken. Her book *The Broken Image,* marked the beginning of healing and restoration for countless individuals, while her *Real Presence* has ushered many into a profound sense of the presence of God and the healing that flows from it.[87]

Like Cullis and Simpson in the nineteenth century, those healed under Payne have gone on to lead their own healing ministries. Mario Bergner was healed by Payne's ministry. His book *Setting Love in Order* has reached thousands caught in the bonds of sexual sin, and ministry has been the source of healing and freedom for many.[88]

John Wimber, the founder of the Vineyard movement, brought new attention to the importance of healing in his books (with Kevin Springer) *Power Evangelism* and *Power Healing,* both of which stemmed from class notes for a now famous 1983–84 course at Fuller Theological Seminary, "MC510."[89] Wimber's insight—which is essentially that the Holy Spirit is alive and well and willing to touch people today just as He was in the earliest church—is foundational to the training and teaching of the Vineyard's ministry. Randy Fisk, a Vineyard pastor who helped train and guide our teams, incorporates many of these insights and methods into a series of excellent books.

Other works on healing have appeared in the popular press, two of which already mentioned: *Love, Medicine and Miracles* and *Healing Words.* Much of the recent interest in *Love, Medicine and Miracles* stems from Dr. Bernie Siegel's own healing and his subsequent writing and promotion of spiritual alternatives to modern medicine. Larry Dossey's *Healing Words*, a *New York Times* best-seller, focuses on the value and importance of prayer in conjunction with medicine.

Hundreds of other books on healing have been written over the last century. From many denominations and faith traditions, they virtually all converge on one simple realization: God still heals, and we access His healing power

---

[86] Francis MacNutt, *Healing*; and *Deliverance from Evil Spirits.*
[87] Leanne Payne, *Real Presence: The Glory of Christ With Us and Within Us.*
[88] Mario Bergner, *Setting Love in Order.*
[89] John Wimber and Kevin Springer, *Power Evangelism* and *Power Healing.*

through prayer. This insight is unavoidable and is foundational to all healing ministries.

However, only a few authors and healing ministries have much to say on the subject of healing for the Woeful (also known as the *Han*, a category devised by Andrew Park). This has been an area of intense focus in our ministry and training in healing prayer, and because of the absence of material on it, significant effort has gone into discovering resources and creating training manuals. The materials of Rita Bennett and Ed Smith are helpful sources in such ministry, as are three books previously cited: *Bait of Satan*, *Embodying Forgiveness*, and *God and the Victim*.

THEORETICAL CONSTRUCTS

What, then, is the theoretical and theological underpinning of a healing ministry? The National Council of Churches asked several leading healers this question.[90] Their replies included:

- "The theology of healing is based upon the sacramental nature of all creation. In proportion to the wholeness which comes to the soul by the operation of the Holy Ghost, the body and mind express that wholeness... [the means are:] the Holy Ghost, the Lord and Giver of Life."[91]
- "I believe that God does heal through Jesus Christ—that it is a result of our faith in Him that God would have us whole.... The actual dynamic in the healing process is a test of our faith, complete trust in God so that one lets go our own anxieties and is completely willing to let God do for him as He wills."
- "Granted that God's will for us is 'wholeness'—salvation of personality—it thus follows that body, spirit and mind are an indivisible entity of integration, and that Holy Unction through the Laying on of Hands is one of the several channels for the enriching and deepening of the 'wholeness.' ... Since we are all spiritual beings whose souls are housed in a temple of flesh, it follows that sacramental means of grace are the most efficacious. As in the Incarnation itself, pure spirit is mediated through sacramental channels, outward in character but inward in result."
- "In expressed need on the part of the individual seeking healing, and faith in God's willingness or readiness to heal according to His will...[the

---

[90] Oursler, *The Healing Power of Faith*, 154.
[91] Here, *sacramental* is defined as "an outward and visible sign of an inward and spiritual grace." That is, it is not about ritual or liturgy, but about what can be seen physically as a sign of a spiritual change.

means are:] Faith, of course; however, certainly in conjunction with faith in the physician as well as the Divine."

- "I believe that our Lord meant what He said when He told His Church to preach, to teach, and to heal. Because the Church is our Lord's body on earth, His life and His power are mediated through the Church. ... [The means are:] (a) Faith in God through Christ upon the part of the one who is doing the ministering. (b) A willingness to be healed by the ones who are being ministered to. (c) Faith on their part when they know they are being prayed for."

The source of the power of prayer for healing is not in the one who prays, but in the Spirit of God. As John Maillard put it:

> Remember that prayer is a channel which God uses. There is nothing of mere human power in prayer. The only part that is human is the channel. Just as the bed and banks of a river are a channel formed of earth for water to flow through, so our prayers are a channel formed of faith for the power and love of God to flow through.[92]

Other studies consistently reinforce this concept, even those neither specifically Christian nor even focused on healing. Emmett L. Jones found that prayer is "definitely associated with psychological well-being," and he encouraged psychologists to recognize its importance in therapy.[93] Cyndi Walker found a strong correlation between consistency of prayer, belief in its healing power, and longevity.[94] This is part and parcel of the prayer training conducted by our teams, both in reference to the healing of those being prayed for, and in the spiritual readiness and willingness of the prayer team members (see *Chapter 8: Guidelines and Cautions*).

Rebecca Norris noted the understanding across faiths of the importance of prayer that goes beyond the mere speaking of words and brings the experience of God: "The deeper the stage of prayer, the more embodied the experience. In other words, a trained, disciplined, or purified body is capable of a more interior or transcendental state of prayer ... although language [in prayer] in contemporary times is mainly cerebral."[95] This is borne out in healing-prayer training by teaching that such *prayer invites God, does not dwell on detail, counseling, or advice, and does not fear silence. That is, healing prayer is wholly and unconditionally dependent on God as we are touched and changed by the ministry of the Holy Spirit. We*

[92] John Maillard, *Healing in the Name of Jesus*, 228.
[93] Emmett L. Jones, "A Study of Traditional Prayer, Inner Healing Prayer and Psychological Well-Being Among Evangelical Christians" (Ph.D. diss., California School of Professional Psychology, 1998), 104.
[94] Cyndi C. Walker, "The Practice of Prayer for Healing Purposes Among Older Adults in a Rural County" (M.S. thesis, Texas A&M University, 2000), 48.
[95] Rebecca Sachs Norris, "The Body in Prayer: A Comparative Study" (Ph.D. diss., Boston University, 1999), 85–86.

do not command or direct the Spirit's intervention, but we do seek it confidently, remembering Jesus' words:

> "So I say to you, ask, and it will be given to you; seek, and you will find; knock, and it will be opened to you. For everyone who asks receives, and he who seeks finds, and to him who knocks it will be opened. If a son asks for bread from any father among you, will he give him a stone? Or if he asks for a fish, will he give him a serpent instead of a fish? Or if he asks for an egg, will he offer him a scorpion? If you then, being evil, know how to give good gifts to your children, how much more will your heavenly Father give the Holy Spirit to those who ask Him." And He was casting out a demon, and it was mute. So it was, when the demon had gone out, that the mute spoke; and the multitudes marveled. (Luke 11:9–14)

Here is both the promise of the power of the Holy Spirit to the followers of Jesus and an immediate demonstration of the Spirit's power to drive out a demon and heal the one who had been oppressed.

Further, such healing prayer is humble and plain in its requests, much like the pattern of prayer taught by Clement:

> This also, again, is suitable and right and comely for those who are brethren in Christ, that they should visit those who are harassed by evil spirits, and pray and pronounce adjurations over them, intelligently, offering such prayer as is acceptable before God; not with a multitude of fine words, well prepared and arranged, so that they may appear to men eloquent and of a good memory. Such men are "like a sounding pipe, or a tinkling cymbal;" and they bring no help to those over whom they make their adjurations; but they speak with terrible words, and affright people, but do not act with true faith, according to the teaching of our Lord, who hath said: "This kind goeth not out but by fasting and prayer," offered unceasingly and with earnest mind. And let them holily ask and beg of God, with cheerfulness and all circumspection and purity, without hatred and without malice. In this way let us approach a brother or a sister who is sick, and visit them in a way that is right, without guile, and without covetousness, and without noise, and without talkativeness, and without such behaviour as is alien from the fear of God, and without haughtiness, but with the meek and lowly spirit of Christ.[96]

Spurgeon, nearly two millennia later, agreed with Clement about the worthlessness of formalism in private and public prayer, which was "too artificial to be worthy."[97] On the other hand, he believed God would act

---

[96] Clement, *The First Epistle of the Blessed Clement*, 59. Some biblical scholars believe this letter is genuine and from Clement's hand; others say it is from a later date. Either way, it is a powerful testimony and instruction.
[97] Kevin W. Regal, "Charles H. Spurgeon's Theology of Prayer" (Master of Theology Thesis, Southern Baptist Theological Seminary, 2000), 40.

111

in response to the fervent prayers of believers.[98] In her dissertation on inner healing prayer, Clare Ten Eyck makes a similar point about technique in asserting that genuine "religious experience, prayer, meditation and Inner Healing Prayer are *not just techniques [but] ways of relating to God.*"[99]

The final area of focus in the theoretical construct of teaching healing prayer is the submitted life of the person who prays for healing. James teaches: "Confess your trespasses to one another, and pray for one another, that you may be healed. The effective, fervent prayer of a righteous man avails much" (James 5:16). This is because one who is righteous acts within the will of God. Randy Clark, author of *Authority to Heal* (and numerous other books on healing), makes the issue clear:

> Throughout my research and over the course of my life, I have found too often God is perceived as unwilling to heal because of a misunderstanding of His divine sovereignty. God's will *is* healing. The deeper issue is more often a widely held theology of unbelief, which causes a lowered expectation to receive healing.[100]

That is, when we doubt God's willingness to heal, we disengage, we refuse what is offered freely: "If we have any bodily ailment, we contrive everything possible to be rid of what pains us. Yet when our soul is ailing, we delay and draw back. For this reason we are not delivered from bodily ailments. The indispensable corrective has become for us secondary, while the dispensable secondary matters seem indispensable. While we leave unattended the fountain of our ills, we still hope to have the streams unpolluted."[101] The healing that proceeds from the Lord by the Holy Spirit, of whatever kinds (physical, emotional, spiritual) leads to deeper intimacy with Him, which is always His purpose and goal.

> We are not allowed to sink into sordidness without many a struggle ... once virtue hath gone forth from Christ and come into us, we cannot easily shake him off and his influence over us. How often in wakeful nights, in quiet hours of reverie, in some still moment ... has Christ come back in all his old time beauty, splendor, and power. ... Then again the heavens open their brassy skies, earthly passions fade away, and God is seen to be all-in-all.[102]

---

[98] Ibid., 9.
[99] Clare Catherine Rossiter Ten Eyck, "Inner Healing Prayer: The Therapist's Perspective" (Ed.D. diss., University of South Dakota, 1993), 30.
[100] Randy Clark, *Authority to Heal*, 48.
[101] John Chrysostom, *The Gospel of Matthew, Homily 14.3*, ed. Manlio Simonetti, in *Ancient Christian Commentary on Scripture: Old Testament*, 1A:74–75.
[102] John Jabez Lanier, *Why I Am a Christian*, 111.

The prayer offered in faith has a certain lack of anxiety in it, however earnest it may be: "Therefore I say to you, whatever things you ask when you pray, believe that you receive them, and you will have them" (Mark 11:24). Of this Scripture it has been said:

> This is prayer in union with God; the very petition has been inspired by God, that our desire to receive may meet His desire to give; and that prayer can never fall to the ground.... We may not see how the answer is coming, but faith rests in God and waits patiently in Him without an anxious thought or doubt, for He is directing all things towards the fulfillment of His Will, and will guide us in our co-operation with Him until the work is accomplished.[103]

Jesus demonstrated this quiet but confident spirit. Cyril of Alexandria put it this way:

> John, "while he was preaching the baptism of repentance," offered himself as a model for those who were obliged to lament, whereas the Lord "who was preaching the kingdom of heaven" similarly displayed radiant freedom in himself. In this way Jesus outlined for the faithful indescribable joy and an untroubled life. The sweetness of the kingdom of heaven is like a flute. The pain of Gehenna is like a dirge.[104]

That is, that even in our earnest pleas for healing, the inner spirit, connected to the Spirit of God, is confident and untroubled, for God is utterly in control.

The primary purpose and method of this healing-prayer *teaching* is to invite healing for the wounded *and then teach healing prayer to those who are healed*, that they in turn might become healers. Their empathy is for others who have suffered like they themselves, and their testimony is credible to those still wounded and unhealed. Thus the cycle of violence and abuse is transformed into a cycle of healing and freedom. The sins of the fathers are halted, and the blessings are established for a thousand generations.

The purpose of this book is just that: to teach how to do healing prayer, to bring healing to others, and then train those that are healed to be healers as well.

---

[103] James Moore Hickson, *The Healing of Christ in His Church*, 6.
[104] Cyril of Alexandria, *Fragments 142–143*, in *Ancient Christian Commentary on Scripture: Old Testament*, 1A:225.

Appendix C:
Glossary of Terms

Terms used in this book, and their plain, simple definitions.

Anorexia. An eating disorder where individuals fear gaining weight and eat so little that they become very skinny, often dangerously so.

Apocrypha. See *Intertestamental literature*.

Apologetics. A form of theology aimed at defending or explaining religious beliefs.

Apostolic age. The period of time up until the death of the last apostle of Jesus. This is generally assumed to be circa 95 C.E. The "post-apostolic age" is the time since the death of the last apostle.

Ark of God. Also known as the Ark of the Covenant was a wooden chest, covered in gold, that held the tablets of the Ten Commandments, Aaron's staff, and a container of manna.

Athanasian Creed. A statement of faith from the 6th or 7th century, of uncertain authorship, that declares the Father, Son and Holy Spirit are equal and in eternal unity, and that belief in the declarations of this creed is essential for salvation.

Atonement. Payment for an injury or wrong, either by the guilty party, or on behalf of the party, paid either by the perpetrator, or on behalf of the perpetrator. By extension, the redemption (payment) paid on behalf of us by Jesus.

Cessationist. Someone who believes that the gifts of the Holy Spirit, especially the miraculous ones such as healing and prophesy, ended with the death of the last apostle.

Charlatanry. The use of deceit to take advantage of others.

Christian Science. A Christian denomination, founded by Mary Baker Eddy, that believes the healings performed by Jesus and His disciples are accomplished by an understanding or "science" of supernatural reality.

Consubstantiation. Distinguished from *transubstantiation* and *dynamic presence*, this concept is that the true presence of Christ is with or adjacent to the elements of communion, the bread and the wine, but that the elements are not actually *changed* into His body and blood.

Disassociate. To disconnect from one's self, identity, history, emotions and thoughts. Often a symptom of trauma or abuse.

Discerning the spirits. Used in two primary ways: to detect actual spiritual entities, such as demons or angels, and their activity in someone's life and circumstances, or metaphorically, to comprehend the issues and influences that affect a person's health and spiritual state.

Dynamic (or virtual) presence. From Calvin: that at the moment of reception of bread and wine, the power of Christ to save is communicated from Heaven to the person. This was a point between "mere remembrance" and "transubstantiation."

Egregious. Awful, flagrant, very, very bad.

Emmanuel Movement. An extraordinary ministry established in the early 19th century, that combined medicine, psychology, faith and practical aid for those suffering from mental or physical illness or loss.

Emotional wounding. The idea that, like physical injury, emotional abuse can cause injury to an individual, with effects as profound and long-lasting as any physical injury.

Empirical approach. Put simply, fostering insight and solutions based on experience, not just on theory or theology.

Enlightenment epistemology. An approach to understanding and solutions that asserts that it relies on science and reason alone.

Excised. Cut out, removed.

Extirpate. To eliminate, destroy, kill off.

Foreknowledge. To know something before it happens. This can be as simple as knowing when a certain event will take place because someone told you about it in advance, to a prophetic or supernatural knowledge of the future.

Functional deist. A deist is typically a person who believes there is a God, but that He is not involved in the day-to-day lives of individuals. Rather, God created the universe and set it on its course, then ceased interaction with it. A "functional deist" is someone who may affirm a belief in a personal, interactive and involved God, but who behaves as a deist would, neither seeking nor expecting personal contact or involvement from God.

Gehenna. A valley just outside of the old city of Jerusalem, where parents once sacrificed their children to the Canaanite god Molech. At the time of Jesus this was a garbage dump, filled with worms and rodents, with an unrelenting smoldering fire.

Great Commission. Refers generally to the sending by Jesus of His disciples to spread His teachings and commands to the whole world. See Matthew 28:19–20.

Healing oil. Usually olive oil infused with frankincense and balsam sap. Its use today is primarily symbolic, but actually it is believed to promote healing as an astringent and wound cleanser.

Homophobia. By definition, the fear or hatred of homosexuals or homosexuality.

Intertestamental literature. Books written in between the times of the writing of the "old" and "new" testaments. Some Jewish groups and Christian groups consider many of these books to be inspired writings, and include them in their bibles. Others regard them as of lesser quality. These books include Tobit, Wisdom, Ecclesiasticus and Maccabees, and are often collectively referred to as the "Apocrypha," implying doubt about their authenticity.

Intransigence. An unwillingness to change or consider other points of view.

Judeo-Christian. Coming from either Jewish or Christian origins.

Justified (by His blood). The idea that the crucifixion of Jesus, which included His bleeding and death, is accepted by God as just, proper and sufficient payment for our sins.

Kadesh-Barnea. An area in southern Israel where God encountered the Israelites for their sinfulness.

Karma. A term from Hinduism but common in modern language, used to suggest that the universe, or God, will punish the sinner and reward the doer of good deeds.

Lamp of God. An expression used in 1 Samuel 3 to signify being alive. When the lamp goes out, one has died.

Luminaries of church history. Those writers and members of the church, over the centuries, who by their lives and writings have enlightened those around them, and following them, with insights into Scripture and God's purposes.

Manifest (as in the Holy Spirit). The tangible presence of God, experienced by those present, for healing, repentance, forgiveness, salvation, and more. That is, God's presence makes itself felt as *real* in every sense.

Methodism. An 18th-century movement started by John and Charles Wesley, and others, that provided a "method" for presenting God, for the transformation of individuals and society. After the death of the Wesleys this became a denomination known as the "Methodist Church."

Multiple persona. The appearance in one individual of more than one personality or "alters." These seem to manifest in sequence rather than all at once, and at times one of them may seem to be in charge of the others.

Nicene and post-Nicene eras. The first Council of Nicea in 325 C.E. was intended to establish the basics of the Christian faith and to declare out of bounds those ideas that did not fit these basics. The "post-Nicene" era followed this council and is considered to include the years 325–451 B.C.

Omniscience. The idea that God knows and sees everything, past, present and future.

Pagan. A word used loosely to describe anyone who does not affirm the Christian/Jewish God.

Pentecostalism. A movement whose modern form began in the early 20th century, where the Holy Spirit was invited to fill Christians and change them supernaturally, often resulting in falling to the ground and "speaking in tongues."

Philosophical abstraction. An idea without practical, physical reality.

Placebo effect. The phenomenon that belief in the healing power of a medicine, a person, or a supernatural entity, may cause healing simply because one "thinks" that it will.

Post-apostolic age. See *apostolic age*.

Prayer legalism. A rigid adherence to forms or methods of prayer, often with the belief that they are required before God will act on someone's behalf.

Predestination. The idea that an individual's actions and future have been predetermined by God, and no amount of effort or imagination can change them.

Promised Land. The ultimate destination of the Israelites after fleeing Egypt with Moses. A land "flowing with milk and honey," that is, a wonderful land with a wonderful future.

Psychosomatic. The idea that some quite-real symptoms are not the product of a disease process but stem from the brain and imagination. A related phenomena to the *placebo effect*.

Reliquaries. Containers, usually small and of metal with decorations, that contain the actual or imagined parts of a saint or saints, or their possessions, or means of death. These include some which purport to hold a piece of "the true cross."

Revelation. The revealing of a fact or truth, whether of an individual, a nation, or an era.

Rigorous theology. An effort marked by great care and humility, to understand and explain the things of God.

Sacramental. A sacrament is an action or object used to signify something sacred. Religious garments, decorations, furniture and objects are often used to instill a sense of the sacred and of God, and to open individuals to God's presence and power.

Sanctification. The process or event of dedicating someone or something to holiness and conformance to the leading and love of God. Also to attempt to live in obedience to the commands of God.

Scoliosis. A sideways curve of the spine, resulting in pain and a deformity of posture and movement. Most often diagnosed in adolescents.

Sedimentation rate. A blood test for inflammation in the body, commonly used to detect the presence of rheumatoid arthritis.

Self-aggrandizement. Making oneself seem important, powerful or of high ability. Seeking or taking things for oneself, usually to the detriment of others.

Sex trafficking. Selling or renting humans—usually young or powerless—for the sexual satisfaction of others.

Shalom. A Hebrew word normally translated "peace" but that implies much more, including abundance and happiness.

Spiritual abstraction. An idea without practical, physical reality, but relating to God and religion.

Spiritual anthropology. The history of humans and their religious ideas and practices.

Spiritual disease. A debilitating mental or emotional state, brought about by or with a religion or the supernatural.

Subculture. A group within a larger culture (such as America, or baseball, or farming) that has its own distinctive traits by which its members recognize each other and identify themselves.

Substrata. Underlying structure or elements.

Synoptic Gospels. The books of Matthew, Mark and Luke. The name derives from the idea that these three books each contain a "synopsis" of the life and teachings of Jesus. The Gospel of John contains some synopsis but is considered more of a theology than a history.

Tobit. One of the most commonly read books of the Apocrypha.

Total Depravity. The idea, primarily from Calvin, that all humans are utterly "fallen" and sinful, and that even our desire for God requires God's initiation and inspiration.

Transmission (of sin). The idea and observation that sins in one individual can infect and lead others to do the same. An example is that the abuse of a child by a parent will often lead that child to commit the same sins against their children.

Verbatims. A simple record of the actions and words of an encounter between two people.

Vineyard Movement. A religious movement and later a Christian denomination, founded by John Wimber, that emphasized the effectiveness of evangelism when accompanied by healings and the power of the Holy Spirit.

Woeful: a category referring to the sinned against, their state of victimization and oppression, their **Woe**, and the consequences of sin on them, whether caused by an individual or an institution.

Word of Knowledge. One of many of the gifts of the Holy Spirit (see 1 Cor. 13 for a partial list), whose purpose is to strengthen and encourage Jesus' followers. The word of knowledge refers to an individual knowing something supernaturally, without any normal means. See Chapter 1 for an example.

Word of Wisdom. See *Word of Knowledge* for a parallel. The word of Wisdom differs in being God-given counsel for another, rather than knowledge.

Yeshua. The most common Hebrew pronunciation of Jesus' name. "Jesus" is not how He was known or called by those who knew Him. "Yeshua" is the most commonly accepted, though there are other variants that may have been used.

Appendix D:
Bibliography on Healing

Print Publications

Augustine. *City of God*. Garden City, NY: Image Books, 1958.

Augustine, "Sermon 77.3." Ed. Joseph T. Lienhard. Reprinted in *Ancient Christian Commentary on Scripture: Old Testament*, ed. Thomas C. Owen. Downers Grove, IL: InterVarsity Press, 2001.

Bennett, Rita. *You Can Be Emotionally Free*. Gainesville, FL: Bridge-Logos Publishers, 1998.

Bergner, Mario. *Setting Love in Order*. Grand Rapids: Baker, 1995.

Bevere, John. *The Bait of Satan: Your Response Determines Your Future*. Lake Mary, FL: Creation House, 1994.

Carlson, Dwight L. *Why Do Christians Shoot Their Wounded?* Downers Grove, IL: InterVarsity Press, 1994.

Carroll, Charles. *The Tempter of Eve*. St. Louis: Adamic Publishing Co., 1902.

Chrysostom, John. *The Gospel of Matthew, Homily 14.3*. Ed. Manlio Simonetti. Reprinted in Thomas C. Owen, gen. ed., *Ancient Christian Commentary on Scripture: Old Testament*, vol. 1A. Downers Grove, IL: InterVarsity Press, 2001.

———. *Homilies on Acts 4*. Ed. Joseph T. Lienhard. Reprinted in Thomas C. Owen, gen. ed., *Ancient Christian Commentary on Scripture: Old Testament*, vol. 3. Downers Grove, IL: InterVarsity Press, 2001.

Clark, Randy. *Authority to Heal*. Shippensburg, PA: Destiny Image Publishers, 2016.

Clement. *The First Epistle of the Blessed Clement, the Disciple of Peter the Apostle*. Reprinted in A. Cleveland Cox, *The Ante-Nicene Fathers*, vol. 8. Peabody, MA: Hendrickson Publishers, 1995. First published 1896.

Cox, A. Cleveland. *The Apostolic Fathers with Justin Martyr and Irenaeus*. Peabody, MA: Hendrickson Publishers, 1995.

———. *The Ante-Nicene Fathers*. Peabody, MA: Hendrickson Publishers, 1995. First published 1896.

Creswell, John W. *Research Design: Qualitative and Quantitative Approaches*. Thousand Oaks, CA: Sage Publications, 1994.

Cullis, Charles. "Let Go and Trust." Tract published by Willard Tract Depository, n.d. Reprinted in Daniel Steele, *Milestone Papers*. New York: Phillips & Hunt, 1878.

Cyril of Alexandria. *Fragments 142–143*. Ed. Manlio Simonetti. Reprinted in Thomas C. Owen, gen. ed., *Ancient Christian Commentary on Scripture: Old Testament*, vol. 1A. Downers Grove, IL: InterVarsity Press, 2001.

Dossey, Larry. *Healing Words*. New York: Harper Paperbacks, 1993.

———. *Prayer Is Good Medicine*. San Francisco: HarperCollins, 1997.

Elwell, Walter A. *Evangelical Dictionary of Theology*. Grand Rapids: Baker Book House, 1984.

Enright, Robert D. *Forgiveness Is a Choice*. Washington, D.C.: APA LifeTools, 2001.

Freyd, Jennifer J. *Betrayal Trauma*. Cambridge, MA.: Harvard University Press, 1996.

Friesen, James G. *Uncovering the Mystery of MPD*. San Bernadino, CA: Here's Life Publishers, 1991.

Gentile, Ernest B. *Your Sons and Daughters Shall Prophesy*. Grand Rapids: Chosen Books, 1999.

Griffin, John Howard. *Black Like Me*. Boston: Houghton Mifflin Company, 1977. Originally published 1960.

Hammond, Frank and Ida Mae. *Pigs in the Parlor*. Kirkwood, MO: Impact Christian Books, 1990.

Hickson, James Moore. *The Healing of Christ in His Church*. New York: Edwin S. Gorham, 1919.

Jones, L. Gregory. *Embodying Forgiveness: A Theological Analysis*. Grand Rapids: William B. Eerdmans, 1995.

Kearney, R. Timothy. *Caring for Sexually Abused Children: A Handbook for Families and Churches*. Downers Grove, IL: InterVarsity Press, 2001.

Koenig, Harold G. *The Healing Power of Faith*. New York: Simon & Schuster, 1999.

———. Michael E. McCollough, and David B. Larson. *Handbook of Religion and Health*. New York: Oxford University Press, 2001.

Kroeger, Catherine Clark, and Nancy Nason-Clark. *No Place for Abuse*. Downers Grove, IL: InterVarsity Press, 2001.

Lampman, Lisa Barnes, and Michelle D. Shattuck. *God and the Victim*. Grand Rapids: William B. Eerdmans Publishing Co. and Neighbors Who Care, 1999.

Lanier, John Jabez. *Why I Am a Christian*. Fredericksburg, VA: John J. Lanier, Publisher, 1914.

Levin, Jeff. *God, Faith, and Health: Exploring the Spirituality-Healing Connection.* New York: John Wiley & Sons, 2001.

Lewis, C. S. *The Problem of Pain.* San Francisco: HarperSanFrancisco, 1996. Originally published 1940.

Lewis, Sharon Gottfried. *Going Through the Journey of Healing.* Agape Publishing, 2019.

Love, Rick. *Muslims, Magic and the Kingdom of God*. Pasadena: William Carey Library, 2000.

MacNutt, Francis. *Deliverance From Evil Spirits*. Grand Rapids: Chosen Books, 1995.

———. *Healing.* Altamonte Springs, FL: Creation House, 1988.

———. *Overcome by the Spirit.* Grand Rapids: Chosen Books, 1990.

Maillard, John. *Healing in the Name of Jesus: A Book of Devotion*. London: Hodder & Stoughton, 1936.

McCrossan, T. J. *Bodily Healing and the Atonement*. Tulsa: Kenneth Hagin Ministries, 1982.

McCullough, Michael E., Steven J. Sandage, and Everett L. Worthington Jr. *To Forgive Is Human.* Downers Grove, IL: InterVarsity Press, 1997. Originally published 1930.

Meyer, Joyce. *The Root of Rejection.* Tulsa: Harrison House, 1994.

Myers, William R. *Research in Ministry*. Chicago: Exploration Press, 2000.

Oden, Thomas C., gen. ed. *Ancient Christian Commentary on Scripture: Old Testament*. Downers Grove, IL: InterVarsity Press, 2001.

Okholm, Dennis. *The Gospel in Black and White*. Downers Grove, IL: InterVarsity Press, 1997.

Oursler, Will. *The Healing Power of Faith*. New York: Hawthorn Books, Inc., 1957.

Origen. *Against Celsus*. Clement. Reprinted in A. Cleveland Cox, *The Ante-Nicene Fathers*, vol. 4. Peabody, MA: Hendrickson, 1995.

———. *Homilies on Numbers 27:12*. Ed. Joseph T. Lienhard. Reprinted in *Ancient Christian Commentary on Scripture: Old Testament*, vol. 3. Downers Grove, IL: InterVarsity Press, 2001.

———. *Commentary on Matthew*. Reprinted in A. Cleveland Cox, *The Ante-Nicene Fathers,* vol. 9. Peabody, MA: Hendrickson Publishers, 1995. First published 1896.

Park, Andrew Sung, and Susan L. Nelson. *The Other Side of Sin*. Albany, NY: State University of New York Press, 2001.

———. *Racial Conflict and Healing: An Asian-American Theological Perspective*. Maryknoll, NY: Orbis Books, 1996.

———. *The Wounded Heart of God: The Asian Concept of Han and the Christian Doctrine of Sin*. Nashville: Abingdon Press, 1993.

Payne, Leanne. *Real Presence: The Glory of Christ With Us and Within Us*. Grand Rapids,: Baker Books, 1995.

———. *The Broken Image*. Grand Rapids: Baker Books, 1996. First published 1981.

Perkins, Spencer, and Chris Rice. *More Than Equals: Racial Healing for the Sake of the Gospel*. Downers Grove, IL: InterVarsity Press, 2000.

Pinnock, Clark, et al. *The Openness of God*. Downers Grove, IL: InterVarsity Press, 1994.

Plantinga, Cornelius. *Not the Way It's Supposed to Be: A Breviary of Sin*. Grand Rapids: Eerdmans, 1995.

Potter, Ronald C. "Race, Theological Discourse and the Continuing American Dilemma." Reprinted in Dennis Okhom, *The Gospel in Black and White*, Downers Grove, IL: InterVarsity Press, 1997).

Price, Frederick K. C. *Race, Religion and Racism,* 2 vols. Los Angeles: Faith One Publishing, 2001. First published 1960.

Sandford, John and Paula. *Healing the Wounded Spirit.* Tulsa: Victory House, 1985.

———. *The Transformation of the Inner Man.* Tulsa: Victory House, 1982.

Sanford, Agnes. *The Healing Gifts of the Spirit.* San Francisco: Harper & Row, 1966.

———. *The Healing Light.* New York: Ballantine Books, 1947.
Schaff, Philip. *History of the Christian Church,* 8 vols. Grand Rapids: William B. Eerdmans Publishing Co., 1995. Originally published 1910.

Siegel, Bernie S. *Love, Medicine and Miracles.* New York: Harper & Row, 1986.

Sittser, Gerald L. *Loving Across Our Differences*. Downers Grove, IL: InterVarsity Press, 1994.

Smith, Edward M. *Beyond Tolerable Recovery*. Campbellsville, KY: Alathia Publishing, 1996.

Stake, Robert E. *The Art of Case Study Research.* Thousand Oaks, CA: Sage Publications, 1995.

Stone, Bryan P. *Compassionate Ministry: Theological Foundations*. Maryknoll, NY: Orbis Books, 2001.

Synan, Vinson. *The Twentieth-Century Pentecostal Explosion: The Exciting Growth of Pentecostal Churches and Charismatic Renewal Movements.* Altamonte Springs: Creation House, 1987.

Weatherhead, Leslie D. *Psychology, Religion and Healing*. Nashville: Abingdon-Cokesbury Press, 1951.

Whitehead, Alfred N. *Process and Reality.* New York: The Macmillan Company, 1929.

Wilson, Earl, et al. *Restoring the Fallen: A Team Approach to Caring, Confronting and Reconciling.* Downers Grove, IL: InterVarsity Press, 1997.

Wimber, John, and Kevin Springer. *Power Evangelism.* New York: HarperCollins, 1986.

———. *Power Healing.* New York: HarperCollins, 1987.

Theses, Dissertations and Papers

Chappell, Paul Gale. "The Divine Healing Movement in America." Ph.D. diss., Drew University, 1983.

Diebold, Michael Anthony. "The Letter of Pope Innocent I to Decentius of Gubbio, a Translation and Commentary." Master of Arts Thesis, Notre Dame University, 1974.

Eddings, Donnie Rose. "A Seminar Presenting the Team Approach to Prayer for the Psychological, Spiritual and Physical Healing of People in Foursquare Churches in Southern California." D.Min. Applied Research Project, Oral Roberts University, 1997.

Jones, Emmett L. "A Study of Traditional Prayer, Inner Healing Prayer and Psychological Well-Being Among Evangelical Christians." Ph.D. diss., California School of Professional Psychology, 1998.

Koch, George. "Investigative Paper on Fear of the Other." Paper submitted to King's College and Seminary, June 2002.

Norris, Rebecca Sachs. "The Body in Prayer: A Comparative Study." Ph.D. diss., Boston University, 1999.

Regal, Kevin W. "Charles H. Spurgeon's Theology of Prayer." Master of Theology thesis, Southern Baptist Theological Seminary, 2000.

Schlientz, Margaret Anne. "A Study on the Decrease of Unresolved Anger Through a Teaching Protocol and Healing Prayer as a Nursing Intervention in Spiritual Care." Ph.D. diss., University of Pittsburgh, 1981.

Ten Eyck, Clare Catherine Rossiter. "Inner Healing Prayer: The Therapist's Perspective." Ed.D. diss., Univ. of South Dakota, 1993.

Walker, Cyndi C. "The Practice of Prayer for Healing Purposes Among Older Adults in a Rural County." Master of Science thesis, Texas A&M University, 2000.

Internet and Software Resources

Additional resources available at **www.GeorgeKoch.com**

BibleWorks Software for Biblical Exegesis and Research. Electronic edition of the Bible. Bigfork, MT: Hermeneutica, 2001.

Calvin, John. *Institutes of Religion.* trans. Henry Beveridge. https://www.ccel.org/ccel/c/calvin/institutes/cache/institutes.pdf

Charles Finney. *Lectures on Systematic Theology.* ed. J. H. Fairchild. http://truthinheart.com/EarlyOberlinCD/CD/Finney/Theology/stcon.htm

Lee, Joyce, and Glenn Gohr. "Women in the Pentecostal Movement." *Enrichment Journal: A Journal for Pentecostal Ministry.* http://www.ag.org/enrichmentjournal/199904/060_women.cfm

New Advent Catholic Encyclopedia. www.newadvent.org/cathen/07015a.htm

"Spousal Abuse of Men," AFU and Urban Legend Archive. http://www.urbanlegends.com/misc/spousal_abuse_of_men.html

Wesley, John. *Wesley's Notes on the Bible.* Online. Grand Rapids: Christian Classics Ethereal Library, 2010. www.ccel.org/w/wesley/notes

Weyland, Victor J. "An Essay on Faith Healing." www.wls.wels.net/library/Essays/Authors/w/WeylandFaith/WeylandFaith.rtf

"Who is Isa al Masih?" www.isaalmasih.net/isa

Index

www.ingramcontent.com/pod-product-compliance
Lightning Source LLC
LaVergne TN
LVHW061302060426
835510LV00014B/1847